Accompanying, Discerning, Integrating

Accompanying, Discerning, Integrating

A HANDBOOK FOR THE PASTORAL CARE OF THE FAMILY ACCORDING TO *AMORIS LAETITIA*

José Granados
Stephan Kampowski
Juan José Pérez-Soba

Translated by Michael J. Miller

Steubenville, Ohio
www.emmausroad.org

Emmaus Road Publishing
1468 Parkview Circle
Steubenville, Ohio 43952

Printed in the United States of America

Library of Congress Cataloging-in-Publication Data
Names: Granados, Jose, 1970- author.
Title: Accompanying, discerning, integrating : a handbook for pastoral care of the family according to Amoris laetitia / Jose Granados, Stephan Kampowski, and Juan Jose Perez-Soba ; translated by Michael J. Miller.
Other titles: Amoris laetitia. English
Description: Steubenville : Emmaus Road Pub., 2017. | Description based on print version record and CIP data provided by publisher; resource not viewed.
Identifiers: LCCN 2017004613 (print) | LCCN 2017015461 (ebook) | ISBN 9781945125379 (ebook) | ISBN 9781945125362 (pbk.)
Subjects: LCSH: Families--Religious aspects--Catholic Church. | Catholic Church. Pope (2013- : Francis). Amoris laetitia. | Church work with families--Catholic Church. | Catholic Church--Doctrines.
Classification: LCC BX2351 (ebook) | LCC BX2351 .G7213 2017 (print) | DDC 259/.1--dc23
LC record available at https://lccn.loc.gov/2017004613

Cover image: *The Road to Emmaus* (2015) by Daniel Bonnell
Cover design and layout by Margaret Ryland

TABLE OF CONTENTS

INTRODUCTION

THE Apostolic Exhortation *Amoris laetitia* (hereafter, AL) has given rise to different interpretations, and any in-depth study of its theological conclusions will undoubtedly require time and patience. However, since no one can refrain from acting, the practical questions it raises cannot be postponed. Whether it be pastors hearing confessions, bishops giving priests guidelines on pastoral activity, or families working in pastoral care, this handbook is designed specifically for them. The purpose of this guide is to offer sure practical guidelines on the important matter of pastoral care in light of *Amoris laetitia*. At stake in this issue is nothing less than the Church's ability to proclaim the gospel of the family, to offer her light to men and women, to heal wounds, and to build solid sacramental pillars upon which to rest. Also at stake is the vocation of the family to authentic love and the responsibility of priests called to lead their flocks toward the good pastures of life that Jesus has shown us.

We are therefore responding to the Holy Father's invitation: "The complexity of the issues that arose revealed the need for continued open discussion of a number of doctrinal, moral, spiritual, and pastoral questions. The thinking of pastors and theologians, if faithful to the Church, honest, realistic and creative, will help us to achieve greater clarity."[1] An "honest" way of thinking, the Pope goes on to say, means avoiding two extremes, which "range from an immoderate desire for total change without sufficient reflection or grounding, to an attitude that would solve everything by applying general rules or deriving undue conclusions from particular theological considerations" (AL 2). The "greater clarity" that Pope Francis is calling for, compels one to evaluate the reasons for doing one thing rather than another. Certainly, the problems of the family and of pastoral care are not resolved by either resorting to new norms or by making exceptions to old rules. Nevertheless, this "No" to either extreme requires a stronger "Yes," and it is precisely this that is the inspiration for the present manual. It is this "Yes" to the gospel of the family that communicates the light of God and touches the hearts of human beings by enkindling hope in them.

Only fidelity to the gospel of the family gives unity to the Apostolic Exhortation. Without this interpretive key the exhortation would be incoherent and would give rise to internal contradictions between what it says, the sources on which it is based, and the actions it seeks to promote. We are firmly convinced of the coherence of this pastoral conversion to which we are called, and it is precisely this perspective of unity that provides our point of departure in reading the document. If we seek clarity, it is not because of an obsession with doctrine caused by insecurity or by some immature fear of the uncertainties of everyday life. On the contrary, we are in pursuit of the clarity necessary to discern the path along which people's lives mature. This is the clarity of the merciful gaze of the Lord who sets out to teach many things to those who are weary and exhausted, like sheep without a shepherd (cf. Mt 9:36; Mk 6:34).

---

[1] Pope Francis, Apostolic Exhortation on The Joy of Love *Amoris laetitia* (March 19, 2016), 2.

1. WHAT ARE THE CRITERIA THAT ALLOW A COHERENT READING OF *AMORIS LAETITIA*?

Let us start from the need to read the proposal of Pope Francis in a coherent way. An isolated reading of chapter eight that interprets the text out of its context is of no help whatsoever. Instead, this attitude betrays the very lack of reflection against which the Pontiff himself warns. We must therefore point to three aspects of the document's coherence necessary for a faithful reading of the text.

The first is coherence with respect to the Synodal itinerary into which the document fits and which contextualizes it. The continual references to the Synods, which sometimes fill entire paragraphs, clearly indicate that the Pope did not wish to push beyond what the Synods themselves expressed. Francis, in this way, shows his profound conviction in the synodal nature of the Church. One cannot understand this ecclesial undertaking as though it were simply for the purposes of composing a document. Instead, the latter must be read as part of a process. The reference to the Synod Fathers in paragraphs 298–302 confirms this principle of ecclesial coherence. We are not witnessing here a revolutionary Pope bent on dividing the Church with personal but isolated insights. Rather, we have a Pope who wishes to live ecclesial communion to its full extent. His intervention must therefore be understood within the scope of his Petrine ministry in service to the communion of the Church.

The second dimension of coherence is that of the document itself. It would be absurd to interpret a document on the family that puts love at its center by adopting an interpretive key typical of contemporary individualism, such as one based on subjective discernment. It is true that with a document that is so extensive and not always easy, and that is the fruit of long prior reflection, different parts can be observed. Specifically, three compositional styles can be recognized: the first, as has been said, is based on the Synods; the second reiterates Francis' catecheses on the family and St. John Paul II's "Theology of the Body"; in the third, Pope Francis writes without footnotes and offers new ideas. The passages written in the last-mentioned style are precisely the ones that should provide the hermeneutical key to the entire document. They include chapters four and five, which act as the principal points of reference for understanding chapter eight coherently.

The final aspect necessary for reading the document coherently comes to us from the tradition of the Church. Francis himself explains that the Exhortation presents no doctrinal or disciplinary changes, since answers do not always have to be sought along these lines (AL 3). Chapter three is entirely dedicated to compiling the teaching on the family since Vatican II. The unity of doctrine and discipline is still preserved, and it cannot be called into question on the basis of a supposedly "pastoral creativity" that tends to deny it. The citations in the main passages are drawn from *Familiaris consortio* and from the Pontifical Council for the Interpretation of Legislative Texts. Above all, this chapter supports its argumentation with the *Catechism of the Catholic Church* and the *Summa theologiae* of St. Thomas Aquinas. One would have difficulty finding a more "traditional" list of references to be a framework of understanding than this selection by Pope Francis. The principle of continuity is in force. Therefore, when an ambiguous or debatable passage appears in *Amoris laetitia*, the sole valid interpretation is one that reads in continuity with the preceding Magisterium. In no way can the temptation to yield to a hermeneutic (such as the one proposed by Cardinal Walter Kasper, or other theologians, such as Giovanni Cereti) based on some alleged return to a patristic tradition be justified. For this would result in a break from the subsequent tradition. Furthermore, there is no allusion in the document to the Orthodox practice of an *oikonomía* of pastoral tolerance, as Basilio Petrà proposed, or Bernhard Häring even earlier. These are erroneous interpretive approaches that would make the Pope's proposal incoherent.

2. A PATH IN THE LIGHT OF LOVE

The demand for coherence, which has been our point of departure, compels us to propose, as much as possible, some pastoral guidelines that may assist in carrying out concretely the pastoral conversion demanded of us. We must do this without ever forgetting the primordial character of merciful pastoral activity. Pope Francis himself expressed this intention by stating: "Without claiming to present a pastoral plan for the family, I would now like to reflect on some more significant pastoral challenges" (AL 199). Unlike *Familiaris consortio*, which offered direction as to the way pastoral ministry for the family was to be structured in both the universal Church and in episcopal conferences and dioceses, here the Pope limits himself to suggesting general approaches. This demands, on our part, a subsequent reflection of a pastoral nature, which will clarify what paths to follow in order to respond concretely, and in an ecclesial way, to these pastoral opportunities. We think that the experience of the Pontifical John Paul II Institute for Studies on Marriage and Family, which is, at present, on all five continents and therefore profoundly aware of the cultural differences regarding the issue of the family, constitutes added value that can help to achieve this goal.

Pope Francis himself reveals to us the key element of the Apostolic Exhortation when, in chapter four, he quotes St. Paul's hymn to charity: "In a lyrical passage of Saint Paul, we see some of the features of true love" (AL 90; cf. also AL 95). This element becomes readily apparent when one speaks about a love that "rejoices in the right" (1 Cor 13:6). The first section on love, in other words, cannot be considered as a private meditation that is, however beautiful, inconsequential for the question of discernment in difficult cases. On the contrary, following the Synod, the document states that *love*—that is, love between a man and a woman, love until death and open to life, despite everything—is the source of all possible progress. Progress, for every family, "lies in its capacity to love and to teach how to love. For all a family's problems, it can always grow, beginning with love" (AL 53, citing *Relatio* 2015, n. 10).[2]

This is no mere allusion made in passing. In recent years, the truth of love has become more and more important in discerning

---

[2] Synod of Bishops, XIV Ordinary General Assembly, *The Final Report of the Synod of Bishops to the Holy Father, Pope Francis: Relatio Finalis* (October 24, 2015), hereafter, *Relatio* 2015.

actions and in seeing the harmonious integration of their objective and intersubjective aspects. This is why true love must be considered the decisive criterion with respect to the matters presented in chapter eight. The path to follow, therefore, is that of a theology of love, one that, although it must arrive at a pastoral approach, must not succumb to the logic of a technical praxis that must be overcome. The logic of love itself is not content to invent exceptions to rules but always takes into consideration the concrete element of the person who loves, encouraging him in his own life.

We can propose the following excerpt from *Amoris laetitia* 294 as a summary of what has been said, and as a beacon, par excellence, of the whole Apostolic Exhortation (and, in particular, of chapter eight) insofar as its pastoral value is concerned: "This is how Jesus treated the Samaritan woman (cf. Jn 4:1–26): he addressed her desire for true love in order to free her from the darkness in her life and to bring her to the full joy of the Gospel" (AL 294). Jesus starts by turning to the goodness that he sees in the Samaritan woman. This is the goodness sown by God in the heart of every man and woman, which consists in the desire for true love. By addressing this desire, Jesus opens up a path to conversion by leading the woman to acknowledge her wrong decisions and the bad situation she is in. Far from being elements of goodness, or parts of a path toward the Gospel, these decisions and her situation present a major obstacle that prevent her from attaining fullness of life.

One cannot understand Jesus' response to the Samaritan woman as a merely rhetorical statement. It is obviously situated in a "difficult case" in which Christ clearly proposes conversion without making concessions. Above all else, we must keep this in mind, since this passage is the one cited in the paragraph preceding the remark on the "law of gradualness," and is the primary reference point for any genuine process of personal development. In other words, the light of true love must be considered the key to personal discernment.[3] We understand, therefore, that the "de-

---

[3] Cf. AL 295: "This is not a 'gradualness of law' but rather a gradualness in the prudential exercise of free acts on the part of subjects who are not in a position

sire for true love" is the thing that must guide all the Church's activity, for in this desire is found the action of God who draws all things to himself.

3. THE BOND: THE FIRST EXPRESSION OF MERCY AS PASTORAL TRUTH

The light of the truth of love constitutes the basis for any pastoral activity. It also offers the dimension of mercy with which it is necessary to carry it out. In the Apostolic Exhortation, mercy appears as a fruit of love, one connected with "true love."[4] The logic internal to love enables us correctly to incorporate into our moral judgment the necessary condemnation of sin, as well as the invitation to the sinner to convert so that he may grow in fullness of life. It is precisely these two dimensions that structure merciful action because "mercy is the fullness of justice and the most radiant manifestation of God's truth" (AL 311).[5]

Consequently, it is necessary to avoid the merely "tolerant" sense of mercy, which neither eliminates evil nor heals the person, for this only serves to make peace with disorder. Pope Francis is here reminding us of the biblical roots of mercy, whereby "the true meaning of mercy . . . entails the restoration of the covenant" (AL 64).[6] The standard of the divine covenant is God's great mercy, not human frailty. Divine mercy along renders human beings capable of living up to the covenant by healing their wounds and strengthening them anew through the promise of a full life. The Cross teaches us that no human failing is stronger than God's love, a love that conquers sin and death.

From this follows one of the most striking features of the

---

to understand, appreciate, or fully carry out the objective demands of the law."

4 Cf. AL 27: "Love also bears fruit in mercy and forgiveness."

5 This is the sense of mercy intended by AL 310: "This [mercy] is not sheer romanticism or a lukewarm response to God's love, which always seeks what is best for us."

6 Citing Pope John Paul II's Encyclical Letter *Dives in misericordia* (November 30, 1980), n. 4.

whole Apostolic Exhortation: the matrimonial bond is not just considered as a juridical effect but rather as an expression of true love and the primary object of all pastoral care. The statements, along these lines, are very clear: "The pastoral care of engaged and married couples should be centred on the marriage bond, assisting couples not only to deepen their love but also to overcome problems and difficulties" (AL 211). This principle is also stressed later when the bond is defined as the basis for the spiritual life of marriage: "In the end, marital spirituality is a spirituality of the bond, in which divine love dwells" (AL 315). The central role of the bond is also reinforced, since the affirmation of its reality constitutes the very first statement of chapter eight.[7]

From the perspective of love, the marriage bond receives a dynamic sense. The bond becomes the resource that allows the married couple to respond in faithfulness to the different conditions of life, relying on the power of grace. The reader should recognize, in this account of the bond, the imprint of the entire fourth chapter, which concludes with the following statement: "The marriage bond finds new forms of expression and constantly seeks new ways to grow in strength. These both preserve and strengthen the bond. They call for daily effort. None of this, however, is possible without praying to the Holy Spirit for an outpouring of his grace, his supernatural strength and his spiritual fire, to confirm, direct and transform our love in every new situation" (AL 164). Through this grace, married couples draw the strength to continue their journey by responding to God's call to live in fidelity to his gifts. As such, one must be conscious of the fact that "[t]he indissolubility of marriage—'what God has joined together, let no man put asunder' (Mt 19:6)—should not be viewed as a 'yoke' imposed on humanity, but as a 'gift' granted to those who are joined in marriage" (AL 62). This principle re-

[7] Cf. AL 291: "The Synod Fathers stated that, although the Church realizes that any breach of the marriage bond 'is against the will of God', she is also 'conscious of the frailty of many of her children'." The citation is from: Synod of Bishops, III Extraordinary General Assembly, *The Pastoral Challenges of the Family in the Context of Evangelization: Relatio Synodi* (October 18, 2014), n. 24 (hereafter, *Relatio* 2014).

fers Christians to the moral law, which is said to be "a gift of God which points out the way" (AL 295).

4. THE UNITY OF ONE PROCESS: ACCOMPANYING, INTEGRATING, AND DISCERNING

We now have at our disposal several useful criteria with which to specify the pastoral process. Taking the directive of chapter four ("true love") as the central idea of what is called for in chapter eight, these central criteria are, as the Holy Father himself observes, *accompanying, discerning, and integrating*. Since each are to be regarded as necessary for the internal organization of any instance of pastoral care faithful to *Amoris laetitia*, let us approach each in turn.

Accompanying is the initial rapprochement that the Church makes with her children to establish a stable, ongoing rapport. In contrast to any hurried solution of problems, accompaniment is aware of the time needed for the truth of love to mature in the person. It must be made clear that the question of access to the sacraments for any person in an irregular situation can never be understood as a request for an entitlement. No priest or person otherwise in charge can grant permission for such a person to approach the sacraments. This is not what Pope Francis has done and thus no bishop or priest can do so either.

By observing this criterion of accompaniment, which consists of not leaving a person alone, pastoral *discernment* is, in turn, carried out. Pastoral care is never instantaneous but must always observe, realistically, the situation of each person, particularly in cases of great fragility. The law of gradualness, noted as the fundamental criterion of the aforesaid discernment, is not valid without pastoral accompaniment. In no instance can the pastoral caregiver support "the notion that any priest can quickly grant 'exceptions,' or that some people can obtain sacramental privileges in exchange for favours" (AL 300). These excesses are described as "misunderstandings" (AL 300), even as they are proposed by various media outlets and are present in the minds of many people.

As has been noted, the *truth* of the bond must be key to this discernment, which is exactly what the Apostolic Exhortation itself presents as its fundamental criterion (AL 211). It is necessary to take into consideration the specific person and his or her situation, seeking, in each case, reasons for which to act. These reasons are not oppressive norms but rather reveal the logic of true love that dwells in a person's heart. Where there are no reasons, and one acts solely by virtue of subjective intuitions, the door is opened to arbitrariness. This would be a true sin, especially since, in marriage, there are considerations of justice in play. After all, the objectivity of marriage necessarily involves the way in which it protects the weaker party.

Integrating, finally, acts as the perspective for the whole process, particularly insofar as it pertains to "irregular situations" (AL 299). It is necessary to situate this within the broader context of ecclesial communion. The natural end of all human actions is our integration into a communion that has specific goods at its disposal, goods which enrich the person who shares in them. In our case, the end or goal of integration is the truth that orients accompaniment and the reason that illumines discernment. The *sacramental* significance of this is obvious: integration assumes *baptism* as the initial gift that is shared and considers the celebration of the *Eucharist* as the end of the whole process. This occurs when the hallmarks of Jesus' love, a love that is "forever" and "despite everything," are assimilated into one's own life, thus giving up every objective situation of sin.

For reasons intrinsic to the Apostolic Exhortation, discernment is the principle discussed most in chapter eight, whereas notes about accompaniment are much scarcer and almost always appear in citations of the Synods. Clearly, this theme had already been amply represented by the Synods' *Relationes*, and therefore required less extensive commentary. Therefore it seems to us more appropriate to change the order of these principles in our presentation and to conclude with discernment. In this way, accompaniment and integration constitute the suitable framework of any discernment so that it will be truly ecclesial.

5. A PASTORAL VISION

Our goal is to help arrange the indications given in *Amoris laetitia* in a way to present a plausible model of pastoral care. In this regard, it is necessary to recall the instruction that appears in the Exhortation itself, namely that any discernment process must be carried out "according to the teaching of the Church and the guidelines of the bishop" (AL 300, citing *Relatio* 2015, n. 85). This simple sentence conveys, in precise form, the serious responsibility of the bishop and of diocesan pastoral offices and ministries. In fact, such a method of acting has not yet being applied to our dioceses, and it will take a significant period of adaptation in order to do so. Our hope is that these pages might be of some help to this end.

Let us adopt, as a point of reference for our analysis, a diocesan pastoral care in which there is a smooth connection between diocesan structures and parishes, and in which pastoral care for the family is sufficiently present at both levels. With necessary adaptations, this model can also be applied to a consideration of the specific pastoral work of ecclesial movements and family associations.

The following proposals concentrate mainly on the directions found in chapter eight of the Apostolic Exhortation. All the while we will remain within the framework of a pastoral approach to the family in which the family itself is the *principal subject* of its mission in the Church.

In the wake of the publication of *Amoris laetitia,* Pope Francis has commented on different aspects of the Exhortation. He has written private letters to individual bishops or to groups of bishops or answered questions posed to him by journalists. At times his remarks seemed to suggest disparate ways of reading the pontifical text. To interpret these statements, it is important to distinguish between pronouncements that are made in virtue of the Petrine ministry—and thus with the authority received from Jesus, in faithfulness to the Scriptures and the Tradition of the Church—and those affirmations that on account of how they are expressed and communicated are presented as private opinions.

This distinction is necessary in order to respect both the Petrine office and the Pope's freedom of expression. If Francis had to bring his authority into play every time that he speaks, he could not communicate with the spontaneity that he desires. The Holy Father is very conscious of this difference. On different occasions he has emphasized that what he wants to teach is found in his encyclicals and apostolic exhortations.

All this allows us to conclude that until now there has not been any authoritative clarification of *Amoris laetitia* and that the different interviews or particular letters—some published without authorization—do not have magisterial value. Every new papal teaching on this point needs to be expressed with clarity, in a way for there to be no doubt that the authority proper to the Petrine ministry, received from the Lord Jesus, is being exercised. In any case, the general principle remains valid that to be binding, every interpretation of *Amoris laetitia,* even if made by the Pope, must always remain faithful to the words of the Gospel and the constant tradition and teaching of the Church.

6. "OF WHICH MAN ARE WE SPEAKING?"

Lastly, a premise fundamental to this work will guide us throughout. What we have to say evidently presupposes the perspective of the gift of faith. Ultimately, everything depends on the question that St. Pope John Paul II ardently raised in his Encyclical Letter *Veritatis splendor:* "And of *which* man are we speaking? Of man *dominated* by lust or of man *redeemed by Christ?*"[8] The Polish Pope's response is decisive: "This is what is at stake: the *reality* of Christ's redemption. *Christ has redeemed us!* This means that he has given us the possibility of realizing the entire truth of our being."[9] If we think of a different human being or if we do not put our faith in the reality of Christ's redemption, then the very questions that we

[8] Pope John Paul II, Encyclical Letter on The Splendor of Truth *Veritatis splendor,* (August 6, 1993), n. 103.

[9] Ibid.

are raising and the problems that we are discussing will seem incomprehensible. Throughout the entire book we presuppose the truth of the words of St. Paul, who writes: "Do you not know that all of us who have been baptized into Christ Jesus were baptized into his death? We were buried therefore with him by baptism into death, so that as Christ was raised from the dead by the glory of the Father, we too might walk in newness of life" (Rom 6:3–4). How can pastors of souls help their brothers and sisters in the Lord, who have been baptized in Christ, to walk in the newness of life? It is toward the answer of this question that we hope to have made a contribution.

CHAPTER ONE

Accompanying: The Patience of a Path

ACCOMPANIMENT is the first key pastoral element upon which *Amoris laetitia* dwells. It is an expression that may involve some risk, for it is easy to think that the act of accompanying someone is obvious, and that it is enough simply to want to do it to know how to do it. The reality, however, is quite different. The term in fact involves an enormous challenge for our current pastoral care that is designed to offer services and provide a meeting place for groups, but which is ill-equipped to journey patiently with persons on a long-lasting path.

Let us begin by adopting a realistic view, which is to say, one that does not allow itself to be fooled by real or imaginary situations behind which the internal weaknesses of our communities lie hidden. We do not pretend to offer here a complete response to today's great challenges with regards to the family. Pope Francis is perfectly aware of this real situation in our Church, and this is why, when he speaks of accompaniment, he begins by noting a lack. Let us read his words referring to the situation of families in difficulties:

> The answers given to the pre-synodal consultation showed that most people in difficult or critical situations do not seek pastoral assistance, since they do not find it sympathetic, realistic or concerned for individual cases. This should spur us to try to approach marriage crises with greater sensitivity to their burden of hurt and anxiety (AL 234).[1]

We note here an obvious indication of the impoverishment of our pastoral activity. Families do not recognize that the Church can help in difficult moments, and they feel alone in these situations. This is the very opposite of accompaniment: we leave alone persons in a state of fragility, and this leads them ever further from the Church.

Devising a pastoral care of accompaniment means initiating a thoroughgoing pastoral conversion, one which will require significant time in order to be effective. Implementing such a pastoral practice, as expressly requested by *Amoris laetitia*, will not be something that happens immediately. We will have to allow time. The important thing is that this pastoral care be well defined, and that it allow us to make contact with the real lives of people. Let us begin, therefore, by laying the foundations for profound pastoral change.

Someone who does not understand the meaning of accompaniment often professes to give individuals immediate solutions. This is precisely the thinking, for example, of someone who says that we should simply change the discipline of the sacraments. It would seem to be an immediate solution, one that could help avoid a lot of trouble. Indeed, it would seem to solve everything, except, of course, the central problem: that people would still proceed without accompaniment. In reality, this proposal would reduce mercy to a well-intended adaptation of a law that we consider too difficult. This approach, which is basically "legalistic," is

---

[1] He makes the same observation with regret in *Amoris laetitia* 52: "But nowadays who is making an effort to strengthen marriages, to help married couples overcome their problems, to assist them in the work of raising children and, in general, to encourage the stability of the marriage bond?"

foreign to the words of Pope Francis, who is clearly moving in another direction.

"A Church which goes forth"[2] and seeks to encounter persons must, like the Good Shepherd, reflect on the paths it has to offer and on how to assist each one of them so as to guide them on a way of conversion that leads to union with God. The shepherd guides the lost sheep back to the sheepfold and does not leave them alone in the fields at the mercy of the wolves. One cannot speak of accompaniment unless there is an effective ability to journey with persons. This is what they need. If we do not do this, we run the risk of disappointing them, and things will end worse than they began.

Aware of this, Pope Francis defines accompaniment as a central criterion for the pastoral care of the family. This is, by no means, a generic intention that can be satisfied by what we are already doing in ordinary pastoral work. The Holy Father makes this point in compelling terms:

> The Church wishes, with humility and compassion, to reach out to families and "to help each family to discover the best way to overcome any obstacles it encounters." It is not enough to show generic concern for the family in pastoral planning. Enabling families to take up their role as active agents of the family apostolate calls for "an effort at evangelization and catechesis inside the family" (AL 200, citing *Relatio* 2015,[3] n. 56 and n. 89 respectively).

As the Pontiff explicitly states, this is a general principle directed at "each [and every] family." In other words, this is tantamount to considering *the family as the subject of pastoral care.* This must be the main light for everything that will be discussed in this chapter. We need to proceed with a comprehensive pastoral conversion that locates the family at the center of pastoral concerns

[2] Pope Francis, Apostolic Exhortation on The Joy of the Gospel *Evangelii gaudium* (November 24, 2013), n. 24.

[3] *Relatio* 2015.

and activities. In this way, we can also understand how inadequate it is to approach pastoral accompaniment solely with respect to difficult cases, for this would mean falling into a tragic, ideological reductionism.

1. THE FAMILIAL SUBJECT THAT TRANSFORMS THE EMOTIVE SUBJECT

With marriage and the family being such a delicate issue, with so many hurts and sufferings, it is necessary also to acquire the wisdom of a physician who is able to heal. The good intentions of someone who simply wants to lend a hand are not enough. We need the knowledge of a cure, since the infirmities and ailments are serious. Sometimes, when thinking of the Church as a "field hospital" (AL 291), we risk being so overwhelmed by the idea of a multitude of sick people in need of medical attention that we lose the genuine perspective that an expert physician would have in the middle of an epidemic. There is, indeed, an epidemic afflicting our society, one in which fragile, emotive subjects live by understanding sexuality as unbridled pleasure, while, at the same time, experiencing it as an unavoidable necessity imposed on them. In the case of an epidemic, the physician's task is not only to go from one patient to another and apply bandages, but rather to understand the origin of the virus so as to fight it with determination. Otherwise the disease will spread, the patients will multiply, and the response, however earnest, will be increasingly poor and ineffective.

The Apostolic Exhortation *Amoris laetitia* provides a precise initial direction: "To believe that we are good simply because 'we feel good' is a tremendous illusion" (AL 145).[4] This is a perfect

[4] It had already warned against "an extreme individualism which weakens family bonds and ends up considering each member of the family as an isolated unit, leading in some cases to the idea that one's personality is shaped by his or her desires, which are considered absolute" (AL 33, citing *Relatio* 2014, n. 5); the 2015 Synod uses similar language but adds: "which distorts family ties. . . , and thus weakens every family tie" (*Relatio* 2015, n. 5).

description of the so-called *utilitarian emotive subject*, who judges external actions solely according to their utility and who is internally dominated by his or her feelings to the extent of being carried away by them in the formulation of his or her moral judgments (emotive). This is precisely where the great difficulty of contemporary pastoral ministry lies. Emotivism is like a carcinogenic cell that causes metastasis, even among Christians. From this, one can ascertain the reasons why so many Catholics no longer go to Mass because they do not feel like it, or stop praying because they do not feel anything. Likewise, one can understand why so many spouses break up their marriages because they no longer feel in love. This "emotivist" principle is a veritable cancer, one that is particularly debilitating right at the moment when persons seek to give meaning to their lives and take the Gospel as their own, personal light. Whenever a person encounters an obstacle or adversity in her or his faith journey, it makes such a powerful impact that she or he vacillates and loses perspective. This is the greatest challenge we encounter within those whom we approach, and our ordinary pastoral ministry is not capable of responding to it.

As Pope Francis emphasizes, merely repeating doctrine or moral norms is of no use to such persons, since they just "do not feel it." It is necessary, then, to accompany them and to set out on a path with them in order that they may recognize a different light capable of building a life. This way of proceeding is similar to that of the early Church, which had to accompany catechumens for extended periods of time. Indeed, these converts had to make the transition from a pagan life, quite far from the Gospel, to a baptismal covenant with Christ. This occurred, moreover, in a climate of incomprehension and tension with the surrounding culture.

For all these reasons, it is not enough to have a "service-oriented" pastoral ministry that is limited to waiting for persons to come and ask for something that they do not feel they need. We cannot suppose that people will feel they are being summoned if we confine ourselves to offering proposals and announcing them at Masses or in parishes. The reason is obvious: many will "feel" that the thing we are announcing is "foreign" to their lives, and therefore meaningless. Breaking out of this limited circle of supply and demand means taking up what Blessed Paul VI had called for in his time, the proclamation of the *kerygma*.[5] This is one of the key points of the new evangelization. Now, however, with the novelty of *Amoris laetitia*, we are being asked to take a further step forward by incorporating persons into a process in which the whole ecclesial community, as the maternal womb of the Church, is involved in nurturing God's children in the Christian life.

2. JESUS CHRIST TEACHES US TO ACCOMPANY

The first step is to understand that accompaniment does not just mean adopting a strategy of moving closer to the world. On the contrary, *it is about starting with the methodology that Jesus Christ himself adopted in order to meet us as it were by accident and to show us the way to the Father.* He, as Master, is the one who teaches us the art of accompaniment through which true disciples are formed.[6] Recall, for example, how he accompanied his disciples on the road to Emmaus after the Resurrection (Lk 24:13–33), showing us the points of reference for every common journey: the Word of God, the sacraments, and communion with the Church, all represented by the Cenacle to which the two disciples returned later that night. The Risen Christ "goes before" the apostles (cf. Mk 16:7), opening paths for them by which to encounter all human beings. His Kingdom consists in the reality of personal relations that always begin quietly, but then proceeds with an internal vitality capable of changing the world.

---

5 Pope Paul VI, Apostolic Exhortation On Evangelization in the Modern World *Evangelii nuntiandi* (December 8, 1975), n. 22. Pope Francis insists on this with respect to families: "In and among families, the Gospel message should always resound; the core of that message, the kerygma, is what is 'most beautiful, most excellent, most appealing and at the same time most necessary.' This message 'has to occupy the centre of all evangelizing activity'" (AL 58). The citations are from *Evangelii gaudium*, n. 35 and n. 164 respectively.

6 Cf. Francis, *Evangelii gaudium*, n. 171: "Today more than ever we need men and women who, on the basis of their experience of accompanying others, are familiar with processes which call for prudence, understanding, patience and docility to the Spirit, so that they can protect the sheep from wolves who would scatter the flock."

Accompanying, therefore, is a specific way of proclaiming the Gospel that is intrinsically connected with following the Master. Recall what St. Pope John Paul II used to say: "Following Christ is thus the essential and primordial foundation of Christian morality; just as the people of Israel followed God who led them through the desert towards the Promised Land (cf. Ex 13:21), so every disciple must follow Jesus, towards whom he is drawn by the Father himself (cf. Jn 6:44)."[7] At stake here is the existential bond with the person of Jesus Christ, on the basis of which the meaning of norms and ideas is understood.

To be sure, this principle was present at the last two Synods inasmuch as they intended to highlight the Christological foundation of pastoral conversion. It is always necessary to begin with the look of Jesus, and the way he "looked upon the women and men whom he met with love and tenderness, accompanying their steps in truth, patience and mercy as he proclaimed the demands of the Kingdom of God" (*Relatio* 2014, n. 12, cited in AL 60, also cited in *Relatio* 2015, n. 37). The Synod is referring here to the famous scene when Jesus looked at the crowds with mercy: "When he saw the crowds, he had compassion for them, because they were harassed and helpless, like sheep without a shepherd," and he has his disciples ask the Lord to send "laborers into his harvest" (Mt 9:36, 38). In this look we see the primary source upon which we must draw for all pastoral concern by the Church.

3. ACCOMPANYING IN TRUE LOVE

Pope Francis expresses the Christian principle of accompaniment with characteristic forcefulness and great precision: I never tire of repeating those words of Benedict XVI which take us to the very heart of the Gospel: "Being a Christian is not the result of an ethical choice or a lofty idea, but the encounter with an event, a

---

7 John Paul II, *Veritatis splendor*, n. 19.

person, which gives life a new horizon and a decisive direction."[8] These words lead "to the heart of the Gospel," from whose "basic core, what shines forth is the beauty of the saving love of God made manifest in Jesus Christ who died and rose from the dead."[9] Accompaniment, therefore, is about the true love that Christ offers, one "possessed of its own logic."[10] It is a love that springs from an encounter and seeks a companion with whom to travel.

Accompaniment in coming to recognize the truth of a love and in the growth and maturity of that love: this is the principle of Christian life. We must keep this firmly in mind, since pastoral care is often understood differently. In truth, this look corresponds to the most profound aspect of the Good Shepherd: "I came that they may have life, and have it abundantly" (Jn 10:10). Along these lines, *Amoris laetitia* is of assistance by presenting the prototype of Jesus' encounter with the Samaritan woman as the model to follow. This instance of pastoral accompaniment is of critical importance, for it is a "difficult case" in which the initial odds speak against its success on account of the radical difference between the two speakers (i.e., man/woman, Jew/Samaritan, religious life/indifference, moral rectitude/utter disorder). But Jesus' accompaniment is able to overcome these obstacles, and the Samaritan woman's life is so transformed that she becomes the first apostle mentioned in the Gospel of St. John. Let us consider the words of the Argentine Pope with respect to the accompaniment of such persons and couples:

> "These couples need to be welcomed and guided patiently and discreetly." That is how Jesus treated the Samaritan woman (cf. John 4:1–26): he addressed her desire for true love, in order to free her from the darkness of her life and to bring her to the full joy of the Gospel (AL 294).[11]

---

[8] Francis, *Evangelii gaudium*, n. 7. The internal citation is from Pope Benedict XVI, Encyclical Letter on God Is Love *Deus Caritas Est* (December 25, 2005), n. 1.

[9] Francis, *Evangelii gaudium*, n. 36.

[10] Pope Francis, Encyclical Letter on The Light of Faith *Lumen fidei* (June 29, 2013), n. 27.

[11] The internal citation is taken from *Relatio* 2014, n. 43.

In the first place, the Pontiff is referring to a process in which the "welcome" is only an initial phase, something important but not itself sufficient. In other words, it is imperative that one welcomes *in order to accompany*. It is this pastoral intention that must guide the first encounter. In the second place, the logic of accompaniment begins with the "desire for true love." The truth of love marks the path, and one must rely on this truth if obstacles are to be overcome and fullness attained. It is necessary, therefore, to adopt the following three main themes as essential to the pastoral approach that Pope Francis is calling for.

First, *true love is the central idea of any kind of accompaniment*. This is a lifelong task which is not simply accomplished by assimilating doctrine and internalizing commandments. It is necessary to cultivate personal relationships: these relationships are the setting in which *following Christ* takes on the contours of existential self-realization; only love provides a suitable framework for understanding what this entails. The specific requirements of true love must be adopted in order for authentic accompaniment to occur. Only by living with the person, and by conversing and handing on convictions, is the meaning of life communicated.

Second, *the journey of accompaniment is one connected with the specific desire of the human heart*. This is why it is necessary to meditate deeply on what the Apostolic Exhortation calls "the world of emotions" (AL 143–146). There is only one way of responding to the "emotive subject" of whom we have spoken about. One need not convince a person of a lot of ideas or commandments to transform him or her into a Christian subject. It is instead necessary to educate her or his desires with respect to the light of love.

We can observe, along with Pope Francis, that this "education of desire" is in no way subjectivist. This can be demonstrated by considering the importance of desire in the *Summa theologiae* of St. Thomas, where it occupies about a third of the treatise on fundamental moral theology (I–II, qq. 22–48).[12] According to Aquinas' realistic conception, the "affections" or "passions" refer to the

[12] Note the references to this section of the *Summa* in *Amoris laetitia*, notes 140 and 141.

manner in which reality strikes us and compels us to act. All human beings have practically the same desires that unite us interiorly. The enormous diversity of human emotions springs from the profound unity of the affective dynamism found in human persons. There is a language of the affections (emotion) that is essential to human communication, and its basic lines can be known. To learn this language requires specific formation, something which must be considered the most urgent of all pastoral tasks.

The goal of the education of desire is affective maturity, which is ever so crucial when it comes to freely choosing one's state of life. This is what Pope Francis is calling for:

> If a passion accompanies a free act, it can manifest the depth of that act. Marital love strives to ensure that one's entire emotional life benefits the family as a whole and stands at the service of its common life. A family is mature when the emotional life of its members becomes a form of sensitivity that neither stifles nor obscures great decisions and values, but rather follows each one's freedom, springs from it, enriches, perfects and harmonizes it in the service of all (AL 146).

Everything that appears later in the document regarding the "extenuating circumstances" that concern the moral act (AL 301–303) has a lot to do with the integration of the emotions. Whenever such integration is lacking, persons are less free and less responsible for their actions. In these cases, it is not enough simply to excuse bad behavior on account of an impaired freedom. Rather, one must urgently discern the need for affective integration. People can always grow in this integration, so long as they are accompanied and not abandoned to their limits and frailties. This is an aspect of hope that St. Thomas always associated with the specific accompaniment of friendship: "For what we do by means of our friends, is done, in a sense, by ourselves."[13]

[13] Thomas Aquinas, *Summa theologiae*, I–II, q. 5, a. 5, ad 1, citing Aristotle, *Nicomachean Ethics*, III, 3.

The third principle implied by Jesus' accompaniment of the Samaritan woman is that of *an accompaniment that is sacramental,* with all that this entails in relation to the source of grace and the action of Jesus Christ in human persons. St. Pope John Paul II insisted on such a sacramental meaning of Christian discipleship—one built on Baptism and the Eucharist[14]—, in order to distinguish it clearly from a merely sentimental understanding. Pope Francis now makes this claim specifically with respect to the Sacrament of Matrimony:

> The sacrament is not a "thing" or a "power", for in it Christ himself "now encounters Christian spouses through the sacrament of Matrimony (LG 11 §2; cf. LG 41 and GS 48). He dwells with them, gives them the strength to take up their crosses and so follow him, to rise again after they have fallen, to forgive one another, to bear one another's burdens" (AL 73).[15]

As we will see in subsequent chapters, an appreciation of Christ's sacramental presence in a marriage is essential for ecclesial integration and for discerning the marital bond. Above all, true love situates accompaniment within a well-defined path that helps orient us in the midst of a multitude of cases that seem so different from each other. There is, in other words, a beginning, which is Baptism, and an end, which is full participation in the life of the Church through the Eucharist. The former establishes a belonging that calls for accompaniment, whereas the latter shows a communion that acts as the end of all actions and manifests the fullness of the Church. The human act that defeats sin and allows us to grasp the reality of pastoral accompaniment is conversion. One can see this in the case of the Samaritan woman. After kin-

---

[14] Cf. John Paul II, *Veritatis splendor*, n. 21: "By the work of the Spirit, Baptism radically configures the faithful to Christ in the Paschal Mystery of death and resurrection; it 'clothes him' in Christ. . . . Sharing in the *Eucharist*, the sacrament of the New Covenant, is the culmination of our assimilation to Christ, the source of 'eternal life.'"

[15] The internal citation is from the *Catechism of the Catholic Church* 1642.

dling a desire for living water in her, Christ asks for a profound change of life, one that leads her to leave her wretched situation. There is no true Christian love without conversion to the love of Christ, a conversion that only arises from the Gospel's core proclamation of redemption from sin (cf. Mk 1:15; AL 297). We must never forget the words of Blessed Paul VI about Christian life and evangelization: "But above all each individual gains . . . [the Kingdom and salvation] through a total interior renewal which the Gospel calls *metanoia*; it is a radical conversion, a profound change of mind and heart."[16] This is the specific task that the Church carries out as Mother.[17]

Into this context, the way in which the Samaritan woman follows Christ fits well, as is indicated by the Synod when it says:

> This clearly appears in the meetings with the Samaritan woman (cf. John 4:1–30) and the adulteress (cf. John 8:1–11), in which the perception of sin is awakened by Jesus' gratuitous act of love. Conversion "is an ongoing task for the whole Church who, embracing sinners, (is) at once holy and always in need of purification, (and) follows constantly the path of penance and renewal. This endeavour of conversion is not just a human work. It is the movement of a 'contrite heart,' drawn and moved by grace to respond to the merciful love of God, who loved us first" (*CCC*, 1428). God gratuitously forgives those who are open to the action of his grace, which takes place through repentance, combined with the intention of living life according to God's will, the effect of his mercy by which he reconciles us to himself. God puts in our hearts the ability

---

[16] Paul VI, *Evangelii nuntiandi*, n. 10.

[17] Cf. Francis, *Evangelii gaudium*, n. 14: "A second area [we can mention] is that of 'the baptized whose lives do not reflect the demands of Baptism,' who lack a meaningful relationship to the Church and no longer experience the consolation born of faith. The Church, in her maternal concern, tries to help them experience a conversion which will restore the joy of faith to their hearts and inspire a commitment to the Gospel." The internal citation is from Benedict XVI, *Homily at Mass for the Conclusion of the XIII Ordinary Assembly of the Synod of Bishops* (October 28, 2012).

> to follow Christ by imitating him (*Relatio* 2015, n. 41; the first part of this citation appears in AL 64).

Such a passage presents us with the profound tragedy of someone who feels enslaved by sin, but at the same time shows the magnificence of a grace that cleanses and heals wounds. In order to understand the change of mind that this requires, it is necessary to consider one essential aspect of true love: it consists not of doing things but rather in responding to a beauty that calls to us. We must develop people's sensitivity to this:

> Proclaiming Christ means showing that to believe in and to follow him is not only something right and true, but also something beautiful, capable of filling life with new splendour and profound joy, even in the midst of difficulties. Every expression of true beauty can thus be acknowledged as a path leading to an encounter with the Lord Jesus.[18]

4. THE FAMILY, THE FIRST PLACE OF ACCOMPANIMENT

In accompaniment, it is necessary to overcome the usual idea of pastoral care defined in excessively clerical terms. Indeed, it is often thought that priests are the only ones who accompany persons. In fact, this is not the case: the first place in which we are accompanied is the family. It is normally our mother's hand that first accompanies us to Mass and helps us, in a loving, maternal way, to know the Church and the faith that enlightens us.

Pope Francis is perfectly aware of this: "Families cannot help but be places of support, guidance and direction, however much they may have to rethink their methods and discover new resources. Parents need to consider what they want their children to be exposed to" (AL 260). In the first place, this is about giving love and allowing it to grow in the unique, common life of the family.

[18] Francis, *Evangelii gaudium*, n. 167.

In the family, faith finds a natural place in which to be transmitted and strengthened and is immersed in an atmosphere of freedom that is typical of true love: "Parents desirous of nurturing the faith of their children are sensitive to their patterns of growth, for they know that spiritual experience is not imposed but freely proposed" (AL 288). This is why the Apostolic Exhortation also shows us the negative process that is observed when there is a lack of natural accompaniment as love grows, particularly when between spouses: "Otherwise, our family life will no longer be a place of understanding, support and encouragement, but rather one of constant tension and mutual criticism" (AL 108).

From this consideration arises the profound conviction that in the pastoral care of the family, it is the family itself that is the subject and active agent of evangelization (AL 200). What this means, concretely, is that we must avail ourselves of families in order to accompany families. This is the missionary vocation of the Christian families (cf. AL 208, 230, 289), which are called by God to accompany those around them in faith and life, offering neighborly assistance and the support of the richness of a family life that is full of God. Without this preliminary step, all the rest is nothing but a series of rhetorical expressions devoid of the necessary support of the concrete ecclesial community.

Many families have already recognized this mission that God entrusts to them, but our diocesan churches do not yet have available a network of families that is sufficiently large to address this task. Moreover, it must be taken into consideration that good will is not enough. Suitable formation is necessary in order to work more readily and responsibly. Now, *Amoris laetitia* addresses such families several times and takes their service to the Church as a given. It upholds, as exemplary, those couples who have matured and gained a certain amount of experience in starting a family, and who are thus ready to accompany others.[19] For engaged

[19] Cf. AL 223: "Pastoral accompaniment needs to go beyond the actual celebration of the sacrament. In this regard, experienced couples have an important role to play"; AL 230: "It could also be helpful to ask older married couples to help younger couples in the neighbourhood by visiting them and offering guidance in the early years of marriage."

couples, and those in the first years of family life, such support is essential.

5. REQUIREMENTS FOR A PASTORAL CARE OF ACCOMPANIMENT

In order to provide a model of accompaniment adapted to all situations, we need to be able to count on families capable of accompanying others. What this means, concretely, is promoting family associations, providing families with Christian formation, and fostering the existence of pastoral care groups in every parish, association, and school. Without such things, accompaniment will be fragmented and selective, and we will not be capable of responding to the great challenge that Pope Francis has set before our eyes. For the Pontiff, all this is clear, and he urges us to act in accordance with specific directions:

> Parishes, movements, schools and other Church institutions can help in a variety of ways to support families and help them grow. These might include: meetings of couples living in the same neighbourhood, brief retreats for couples; talks by experts on concrete issues facing families, marriage counselling, home missionaries who help couples discuss their difficulties and desires, social services dealing with family problems like addiction, infidelity and domestic violence, programmes of spiritual growth, workshops for parents with troubled children and family meetings. The parish office should be prepared to deal helpfully and sensitively with family needs and be able to make referrals, when necessary, to those who can help. There is also the contribution made by groups of married couples that provide assistance as part of their commitment to service, prayer, formation and mutual support. Such groups enable couples to be generous, to assist other families and to share the faith; at the same time they strengthen marriages and help them to grow (AL 229).

Although only an initial outline is presented here, this is clearly a far-reaching pastoral plan that suggests a task of significant scale. One must know that it takes time to arrive at a destination, and that we are talking of sowing a small seed that must grow little by little.

The model to follow may be that of *Caritas Internationalis*, a relief organization that presently has numerous volunteers in many parishes and has, in every diocese and pastoral region, an accessible centralized organization with sufficient means and personnel to help persons in special cases with both initial assistance and personal formation. Moreover, in this charitable association there is smooth, orderly coordination between parochial services and centralized ones, and this allows it to perform its particular role with great efficiency. This is the result of years of work carried out according to a sound approach, and it would be recommendable for this model to be adopted for the pastoral care of the family. Of course, it would be necessary to introduce one important change with respect to the family. One cannot solely concentrate on solving problems, but must instead pay attention to the integral formation of persons, providing them with an education to love. This task indeed belongs specifically to the kind of accompaniment spoken of in this chapter.

In order to promote the growth of parish groups, it has proven effective to organize a formation program designed for parishes. Persons specifically prepared for this purpose could thoroughly explain in practical terms the task of such a group to priests and couples. All this could be done within the framework of an integral understanding of pastoral care for the family. The objective is to form a core group that would then go to expand.

In terms of a more specialized attention to specific cases, it is necessary to organize, in every diocese, Family Guidance Centers designed not merely to be therapeutic but also to evangelize. They should be sufficiently close and valued by parishes, staffed by professionals who have an education and formation relating to issues on the gospel of the family. In this way, such centers would respond to the direction of the document when it says: "Most people . . . appreciate the Church's efforts to offer guidance and counselling in areas related to growth in love, overcoming conflict and raising children" (AL 38). *Amoris laetitia* understands these efforts to be based on accompaniment aimed at promoting the growth of true love, and not just one that seeks to solve problems. It may be more correct, therefore, to speak of "Centers for the Promotion of the Family." It is equally necessary to calculate the expenditures of equipping such an organization with everything that families need. Otherwise we will incur the reproach of the Gospel parable by trying to build a tower without first counting the cost of finishing the work (cf. Lk 14:28).

6. GRADUALNESS: THE LAW OF ACCOMPANIMENT

Once we understand the law as the truth of a path, then we understand that it is necessary to be able to walk. In this sense, the law does not set a limit but rather establishes a direction that must not be lost if we are to avoid losing our way. The law is, in fact, an aid to persons' freedom as they search for life's meaning in their journey towards God. Thus we can understand the role of the law as the principle for all discernment that is necessary for the path:

> In his journey towards God, the One who "alone is good," man must freely do good and avoid evil. But in order to accomplish this he must be able to distinguish good from evil. And this takes place above all thanks to the light of natural reason, the reflection in man of the splendor of God's countenance.[20]

This is a fundamental, positive, and personal task. The Church accompanies human beings, conscious of the fact that "knowledge of God's law in general is certainly necessary, but it is not sufficient: what is essential is a sort of 'connaturality' between

[20] John Paul II, *Veritatis splendor*, n. 42.

man and the true good."[21] One must understand the importance of these considerations to avoid a legalism that would run the risk of suffocating the person's initiative in his or her growth.

With reference to the moral law, there is one particular law that is of singular importance for accompaniment: the "law of gradualness," which refers to a pedagogy of moral conscience that is carried out progressively and that depends on interior dispositions. This law was invoked frequently throughout the Synods' proceedings.[22] It is of fundamental importance to accompaniment so as to embark on a path of following Christ.

It is crucial to have a very clear idea of the evangelical character of the law of gradualness, which has allowed the Church to understand the divine pedagogy and which has led to the classic distinction between the Old and the New Law. The image of the path, which corresponds to the *Torah* of Israel, is taken up by St. Paul when he speaks of the law as the "pedagogue" who accompanies the believer along the path towards the fullness of Christ (cf. Gal 3:24).[23] There is no break between the Law and Christ, but rather a profound continuity through the reception of a new gift. This is what Jesus himself proclaims: "Do not think that I have come to abolish the law and the prophets; I have come not to abolish them but to fulfil them" (Mt 5:17). The revelation of God's grace, which structures the heart and its interior dispositions so as to move the person interiorly, fills the New Law with content, which enables us to live according to the demands of the Gospel.[24]

The precepts of the Decalogue remain forever. Not even love dispenses one from observing them. Indeed, the observance of the commandments is one of the clearest signs of the truth of love: "By this we know that we love the children of God, when we love God and obey his commandments. For this is the love of God, that we keep his commandments. And his commandments

---

[21] Ibid., n. 64.

[22] In *Relatio* 2015, n. 84; AL 293–295.

[23] The lexical form of word "pedagogue" derives from the Greek "*paidos*" and "*agein*" and refers to accompanying a child by taking them by the hand.

[24] Cf. Thomas Aquinas, *Summa theologiae*, I–II, q. 108, art. 1, which is cited in Francis, *Evangelii gaudium*, n. 37.

are not burdensome. For whatever is born of God overcomes the world" (1 Jn 5:2–4). The requirement to observe the commandments is indispensable, allowing for no exceptions. This is what the Church teaches about intrinsically evil acts associated with the negative precepts of the Decalogue.[25]

However, the Church does not teach these requirements without also accompanying persons in their imitation of Christ. The divine pedagogy of grace infinitely opens up human possibilities. Consequently, we must recall the specific moral principle of the logic of true love:

> Love and life according to the Gospel cannot be thought of first and foremost as a kind of precept, because what they demand is beyond man's abilities. They are possible only as a result of a gift of God who heals, restores and transforms the human heart by his grace.[26]

The image of a transformed heart shows us the serious error committed whenever the "law of gradualness" is confused with "gradualness of the law." The latter consists of holding that there are "different degrees or forms of precept in God's law for different individuals and situations."[27] The error lies in adapting the imperative demand of the law to the subjective possibilities of individual persons, which is something that must never be done. It is tantamount to saying that God's law is too rigid for you and that, therefore, another law must be promulgated that is valid in your situation. Such an approach involves making an exception to a moral law, as though it did not apply in a concrete case. Ul-

[25] Cf. John Paul II, *Veritatis splendor*, n. 67: "The negative moral precepts, those prohibiting certain concrete actions or kinds of behavior as intrinsically evil, do not allow for any legitimate exception. They do not leave room, in any morally acceptable way, for the 'creativity' of any contrary determination whatsoever. Once the moral species of an action prohibited by a universal rule is concretely recognized, the only morally good act is that of obeying the moral law and of refraining from the action which it forbids."

[26] Ibid., n. 23.

[27] Pope John Paul II, Post-Synodal Apostolic Exhortation, On the Role of the Christian Family in the Modern World *Familiaris consortio* (November 22, 1981), n. 34.

timately, this means applying another law to this case or softening the same law by reducing the extent of its demands. Pope Francis is very clear in this regard and affirms that there is one moral law that unites all human beings: "The law is itself a gift of God which points out the way, a gift for everyone without exception; it can be followed with the help of grace" (AL 295).

The law is not an external imposition, but rather an interior *path* to the good. From this perspective, saying that there are no exceptions to the one moral law that is valid for everyone is the same as saying that no one is left by the wayside. The proper interpretation of the law of gradualness requires one to understand the law as a path. The point of the law of gradualness is to enable people to stay on track. About all this St. Pope John Paul II clearly states: "In fact 'the law of gradualness,' as it is called, is not possible unless a person sincerely obeys the divine law and seeks those benefits that are protected and promoted by that law."[28] Genuine pastoral care, therefore, is never a matter of dispensing people from a presumably excessive requirement, because not following the law is a damage that brings harm to the human person. With its gravity, sin offends first of all the moral dignity of the one who commits it.

In fact, the common temptation to yield to a so-called "gradualness of the law" has its origins in a legalistic perspective. According to this faulty approach, things would be good merely because they are prescribed by an authority, and it would be the same authority that could also "dispense" from the observance of an excessively burdensome law. Essentially, the good would consist of correctly conforming one's life to an external law, meaning that the merciful care of people would be a matter of "adapting" the law to them, so as to make everything "all right." It is not difficult to appreciate how this represents a significant deterioration of Gospel mercy.

Consequently, any accompaniment or discernment "can never prescind from the Gospel demands of truth and charity, as proposed by the Church" (AL 300, *Relatio* 2015, n. 86). It is necessary

[28] Pope John Paul II, *Speech at the Conclusion of the 1980 Synod on the Family* (October 25, 1980), n. 8.

to understand exactly what this statement demands, what it implies with regards to conversion, and, in particular, how it directly relates to grace. Just as there are no degrees between life and death, so too in Christian conversion—which is a real, true gift to Jesus—there are no degrees between the situation of sin and life in Christ. The Samaritan woman was asked not only to change her life with regard to her cohabitation, but also and above all to acknowledge Christ as the person through whom to adore God in Spirit and in truth (cf. Jn 4:23–24). This was her true life, one which admitted no gradations. Once true life is attained, a person, as with any living creature, begins a path in which growth becomes possible. In the case of the Samaritan woman, this involved becoming a convert and testifying before her fellow townspeople about God. In this growth of a life informed by the light of the law, accompaniment displays its full importance as an aid to the process of promoting human persons.

The above considerations concern the law in the sense in which it was affirmed by the Council of Trent. The Council emphasized the profound importance of the realism of grace:

> No one, however much he be justified, should consider himself exempt from the observance of the commandments [*can. 20*]; and no one should say that the observance of God's commandments is impossible for the man justified—a rash statement censured by the Fathers with anathema [*cann. 18 and 22; cf. *397*]. "For God does not command the impossible, but when he commands he admonishes you to do what you can and to pray for what you cannot do," and he helps you to be able to do it. "His commandments are not burdensome" [*1 Jn 5:3*]; his "yoke is easy and (his) burden light" [*Mt 11:30*].[29]

[29] Council of Trent, *Decree on Justification*, Session VI, chapter 11, *DH* 1536, cited from Heinrich Denzinger, *Compendium of Creeds, Definitions, and Declarations on Matters of Faith and Morals*, 43rd edition, edited by Peter Hünermann [German-Latin edition], Robert Fastiggi, and Anne Englund Nash [English edition] (San Francisco: Ignatius Press, 2012), 380.

The Apostolic Exhortation naturally assumes this dogmatic statement when, in reference to such demands, it declares that "[the law] can be followed with the help of grace" (AL 295). Our knowledge of human frailties and limitations does not lead us to lose this sense of God's fidelity, which is his mercy.

To take human abilities as the measure of God's grace would mean falling into Pelagianism. Here, it is a matter of recognizing the specific, dynamic character of the gift: "What is received depends on the one who receives it."[30] What this implies is that there are two levels to the gift of grace: the level at which the gift is received or rejected, where there are no intermediating degrees; and the level of the manner in which this gift is received, where, by contrast, there can be numerous degrees of variation. The grace of initial conversion arrives as a whole, with a divine measure that proceeds from the reception of a gift: either it is received or it is rejected. But within the scope of its reception, there are numerous gradations, since here we are speaking of the human manner of receiving the divine gift. This is precisely where accompaniment becomes necessary, for someone to journey ahead of us, like the Good Samaritan who takes the wounded man on his shoulders and heals his wounds. By denying the gradualness of the law, one embraces the chief prerequisite for the existence of pastoral accompaniment.

The fact that the non-gradualness of the law is the condition for pastoral accompaniment along a gradual path can be seen in different examples. It is witnessed to by the way in which the first Christians accompanied their catechumens before Baptism. During the catechumenate the truth of the catechumens' conversion was discerned by verifying that they were ready to take upon themselves the demands of an authentic Christian life. Similarly, the non-gradualness of the law was an essential element of Christ's accompaniment of the Samaritan woman. Thus, using her own words, he reminded her that the man with whom she was living "was not her husband" (cf. Jn 4:18). The Jewish people's struggle with idolatry is a further example. They had to travel

[30] Cf. Thomas Aquinas, *I Sent.*, d. 17, q. 1, a. 1, s.c. 1.

along an important path. In fact, Israel was only gradually able to come to a full understanding of the greatness of the one God. At the same time, however, the Chosen People would have *never* been able to arrive at the worship of the one and only God by means of a law adapted to "intermediate forms" of idolatry.

In its positive dimension, the law indicates a path of sanctity that should characterize every pastoral activity:

> All couples are called to holiness in marriage according to the divine plan; and the dignity of this vocation becomes effective when a person is able to respond to the command of God with a serene mind, trusting in divine grace and his own will.[31]

One must always presuppose the presence of grace that makes possible a response informed by charity. Wherever thirst is found, one also discovers "a spring of water welling up to eternal life" (Jn 4:14). Acceptance of a gradualness of the law would destroy the very concept of accompaniment, which has grace as its beginning, conversion as its center, and holiness as its goal. Such is evident in the case of the Samaritan woman who changes her life but, above all, becomes an apostle and witness of Christ. Unless accompaniment begins with grace, centers on conversion, and aims at holiness, it will cease to be a pastoral activity and will become merely a vague kind of solidarity, something indistinguishable from mere human company, and something devoid of any objective. We must insist on the goal of holiness, because this is what marks the whole spirit of pastoral care. The indispensable image of the Church as a field hospital must not be erroneously interpreted as reducing pastoral care to a therapeutic approach addressing the health of persons. Such a pastoral approach is always doomed to failure because it confines God's action within the scope of human limitations. By contrast, it must be made clear that the end of pastoral care must always be *holiness.* Holi-

---

[31] John Paul II, *Speech at the Conclusion of the 1980 Synod on the Family* (October 25, 1980), n. 8.

ness must never be thought as being beyond the reach of persons, even when, like the Samaritan woman, they may seem incapable of it. In this sense, the trust that Pope Francis places in grace is immense: "A married person can experience the highest degree of charity and thus 'reach the perfection which flows from charity, through fidelity to the spirit of those counsels. Such perfection is possible and accessible to every man and woman'" (AL 160).[32] To deny the universal call to holiness is to lose sight of authentic evangelization and discard one of the fundamental principles of the Second Vatican Council.[33] It would be as if someone, seeing that the wine was running short, watered down the better wine so as to give it to everyone, lacking all confidence that grace would bring about a transformation.

The Apostolic Exhortation insists on the concept of "journeying" with grace along a path in which interior change is treated as essential to the conversion of the "hard heart" (cf. Mt 19:8). Such hardness of heart is what prevents a person from living fully according to God's plan, and in reference to this, Francis cites the 2014 Synod: "God's indulgent love always accompanies our human journey; through grace, it heals and transforms hardened hearts, leading them back to the beginning through the way of the cross" (AL 62, *Relatio* 2014, n. 14).[34] As the document subsequently makes clear, this truth is to be applied directly to so-called "irregular" situations:

> The Synod Fathers reached a general consensus, which I support: "In considering a pastoral approach towards people who have contracted a civil marriage, who are divorced and remarried, or simply living together, the Church has the responsibility of helping them understand the divine

---

[32] Citation in footnote 170 of AL: John Paul II, *Catechesis* (April 14, 1982). Cf. AL 316.

[33] Second Vatican Council, Dogmatic Constitution on the Church *Lumen gentium* (November 21, 1964), n. 40.

[34] With a few slight variations and interesting nuances: *Relatio* 2015, n. 41: "Jesus shows how the divine condescendence may accompany the human journey with his grace, transform the hardened heart with his mercy (cf. Ezek 36:26) and guide its fulfilment through the Paschal Mystery."

> pedagogy of grace in their lives and offering them assistance so they can reach the fullness of God's plan for them," something which is always possible by the power of the Holy Spirit (AL 297, citing *Relatio* 2015, n. 25).

The issue is to see the path that the law opens up concretely to assume the truth of its demands, taking into account our limitations. We can observe this more specifically in the section on discernment: "Discernment must help to find possible ways of responding to God and growing in the midst of limits. By thinking that everything is black and white, we sometimes close off the way of grace and of growth, and discourage paths of sanctification which give glory to God" (AL 305).

In order to gradually overcome obstacles in the midst of a pedagogical process of accompaniment, it is once again necessary to adopt the interior logic of love, which accepts desire and guides it. The Holy Father's words enlighten us with respect to this harmonization between the desire of the heart and the requirements of the law: "It is important that discipline not lead to discouragement, but be instead a stimulus to further progress" (AL 270). *Gradualness means embarking on a path of growth, but always beginning with the acceptance of the requirements and consequences of the one law that unites all human beings.* This principle, stated by the Synod and confirmed by the Pope, is so important as to become the hermeneutical key to everything that is subsequently said regarding discernment. The decisive denial of any "gradualness of the law" must be considered the light by which to interpret what is then presented concerning mitigating factors that enter among the circumstances of the moral act (AL 301–303). Under no circumstances can a consideration of such mitigating factors adapt the requirements of the law to what the person considers him- or herself able to do, as though sin could be excused because of weakness. On the contrary, it is a matter of accompanying this initial ability, so that with the power of God's active grace it becomes possible to walk in a life according to the truth of the Gospel, a truth that can in no way be diminished.

From the perspective of pastoral care, one cannot lose the

"possible good" and cease to proclaim the full requirements of the Gospel as anything but *real* and as something that God wants for every person. This, as the document reminds us, is a work of mercy: "'[T]here is a need to accompany with mercy and patience the eventual stages of personal growth as these progressively appear,' making room for 'the Lord's mercy, which spurs us on to do our best'" (AL 308).[35] This is why it is never superfluous to recall the words of Blessed Paul VI in this regard: "To diminish in no way the saving teaching of Christ constitutes an eminent form of charity for souls."[36]

7. THE PROCESS OF ACCOMPANIMENT

In pastoral work, accompaniment should never concentrate on problems, but on persons. Otherwise, we would be experts in resolving difficulties, but incapable of giving life to persons. Pastoral care is not a matter of providing technical assistance, but of forging an ongoing relationship of growth in charity. One clear expression of the wisdom of the Apostolic Exhortation is that it addresses the topic of accompaniment more in chapter six, in the section on general pastoral perspectives, than in chapter eight, which deals with irregular cases. Therefore it is necessary to maintain the subsequent principle: what stands in need of being accompanied is true love, following the natural process of how human beings live it and make it their own. This appears so clearly in *Amoris laetitia* that we must consider it one of its chief pastoral points. The document treats of accompaniment especially in its discussion of proximate marriage preparation and in its reflection on the situation of couples in the first years of their marriage. Here are precisely the two major shortcomings of our current pastoral care of the family. One can appreciate, therefore, why the Holy Father urges us to fill these gaps before all others. The reason is simple. The early years

[35] Citing Francis, *Evangelii gaudium*, n. 44.

[36] Pope Paul VI, Encyclical Letter on Human Life *Humanae vitae* (July 25, 1968), n. 29. The passage was repeated also by John Paul II, *Familiaris consortio*, n. 33.

of a relationship provide the breeding ground for the most serious epidemic afflicting the family.

Our pastoral experience shows us the problem. The greatest infirmity lies in the fact that people getting married very often have a sentimental, romantic idea of love that is highly superficial and little Christian. In addition, they frequently possess an adolescent personality marked by serious defects. These human and spiritual limits quickly emerge in the first years of married life when a couple tries to build a life together. This is where the carcinogenic cell takes root, and it proceeds from there to poison growth and destroy lives. Such shortcomings are the cause of enormous sufferings and must be accompanied with great tact and mercy, always remembering that it is sin—in this case, often infidelity—which is the chief evil that needs to be defeated. In this way one attends to the greatest pastoral challenges of our time, which it is important to understand very clearly.

Nowadays the main difficulty is not divorced persons living in a new union and asking for the sacraments, but rather the large number of couples who have utterly crossed off marriage as a prospect for life. Marriage rates have decreased sharply in Western cultured countries, and the Church has not yet been able to respond adequately to a pastoral problem of such vast proportions. Pope Francis, meanwhile, has invited us to reflect on this fact: "At the risk of oversimplifying, we might say that we live in a culture which pressures young people not to start a family, because they lack possibilities for the future. Yet this same culture presents others with so many options that they too are dissuaded from starting a family" (AL 40).[37] Note that this trend contradicts the desire of persons who, by contrast, desire true love for their lives.

If we read the Apostolic Exhortation with open eyes, we real-

[37] Footnote 14 explains that this is a citation from Francis' *Address to the United States Congress* (September 24, 2015), *L'Osservatore Romano*, English edition (September 26, 2015), p. 7. We can therefore appreciate the great social value that the family has in his view. The thought appeared also in *Relatio* 2015, n. 29: "The Church is concerned at the distrust of many young people towards marriage and is troubled at the haste with which many of the faithful decide to put an end to one marital commitment and establish another."

ize that this is precisely the burning issue with which it wrestles. The document begins as follows:

> The Joy of Love experienced by families is also the joy of the Church. As the Synod Fathers noted, for all the many signs of crisis in the institution of marriage, "the desire to marry and form a family remains vibrant, especially among young people, and this is an inspiration to the Church." As a response to that desire, "the Christian proclamation on the family is good news indeed" (AL 1).[38]

It is necessary to welcome and accept a desire and to accompany this yearning so as to make the seeds of the Gospel grow in people.[39] The specific characteristic of a pedagogy of love consists in helping couples to make sure that their love does not grow in an excessively private or isolated setting, which fosters the merely individualistic interpretations of human sentiment.

On the contrary, it is necessary to give love its proper place in the Church, where it finds a communal setting, characterized by strong ties that spring forth unconditionally from mutual self-giving. This is the yearning and the reason of accompaniment. In this way we will overcome the reductionism of an accompaniment that solely aims at trying to make sure people's situation becomes "regular" again. The clearly legalistic interpretation leads pastors to lose sight of the maturation that takes place in the reception of the gift of true love, which is precisely the thing that structures the process required by the ecclesial society. This shortcoming, unfortunately, is manifest in every pastoral structure that does not presently accompany persons in the maturity of true love, but rather limits itself to offering services in the context of some group dynamic.

---

[38] The citations are from *Relatio* 2014, n. 2 [cf. *Relatio* 2015, n. 2] and *Relatio* 2015, n. 3, respectively. Cf. also: *Relatio* 2015, n. 29: "Many young people continue to see marriage as the great desire of their life and the idea of forming their own family as a fulfilment of their aspirations. Nevertheless, young people, in practice, have varying attitudes with regard to marriage."

[39] Recall the mention of the *semina Verbi* in AL 76.

8. AN INITIAL CONCERN OF ACCOMPANIMENT: MARRIAGE PREPARATION

The first issue to consider is marriage preparation. *Amoris laetitia* insists that there is much more to it than simply being a requirement for receiving a sacrament. Rather, marriage preparation is part of a pastoral care of accompaniment. The main change that is required is that marriage preparation must stop being treated as something marginal: a formation that certain people receive at specific times but which has no impact on the overall pastoral work of the Church. Instead, marriage preparation must become the real, active concern of the whole ecclesial community: "I encourage Christian communities to recognize the great benefit that they themselves receive from supporting engaged couples as they grow in love" (AL 207).

The terminology used by the Apostolic Exhortation must be understood on the basis of the proposal in *Relatio* 2015, number 57:

> In this regard, the three stages indicated in *Familiaris consortio* (cf. 66) need to be borne in mind: remote preparation, which treats the transmission of the faith and Christian values within the family; proximate preparation, which coincides with the various programmes of catechesis and the formative experiences lived within the ecclesial community; and immediate preparation for marriage, which is part of a broader programme, characterized by the vocation to marriage itself.

The change demanded of premarital pastoral care consists above all in moving away from thinking of it in terms of classical catechesis, which is often reduced to an immediate preparation. Although such preparation can welcome people and have some impact on them, it does not arrive at the level of people's deep dispositions, which would be necessary for it to be truly effective. Accompaniment, by contrast, inserts persons into a process of maturation in true love: it is a "pastoral care . . . centred on the marriage bond" (AL 211).

In keeping with the Synod's suggestion, such accompaniment must be carried out by the *ecclesial community*. (In order to be concrete, it is necessary to speak first of all of parish communities, and analogously of ecclesial movements and religious associations.) In other words, the same principle that is proposed for accompanying couples during the first years of their marriage must also be applied to marriage preparation: "The parish is a place where such experienced couples can help younger couples, with the eventual cooperation of associations, ecclesial movements and new communities" (AL 223, citing *Relatio* 2014, n. 40; cf. *Relatio* 2015, n. 60).

Amoris laetitia speaks with great pastoral wisdom about this preparation on two levels: one general, since the common desire of all young people is to learn true love, and the other specific, for those who in fact have become formally engaged.

a. Regarding the Pastoral Care of Young People

With respect to the first level, Pope Francis makes concrete proposals, showing a specific and concrete interest:

> With the help of missionary families, the couple's own families and a variety of pastoral resources, ways should also be found to offer a remote preparation that, by example and good advice, can help their love to grow and mature. Discussion groups and optional talks on a variety of topics of genuine interest to young people can also prove helpful (AL 208).

This certainly suggests a radical change, particularly with respect to the pastoral care of young people. Indeed, it is surprising to note how the enormous pastoral efforts devoted to youths over the past forty years have not led to a rich pastoral care of married people. There has been little positive communication between these two pastoral concerns. Young people have not experienced the Church's attention as a preparation for their marriages, and have consequently not felt the presence of any accompaniment after the celebration of their weddings. This is why the following statement must be read as one aimed specifically at this change in pastoral approach:

> The Synod Fathers stated in a number of ways that we need to help young people discover the dignity and beauty of marriage. They should be helped to perceive the attraction of a complete union that elevates and perfects the social dimension of existence, gives sexuality its deepest meaning, and benefits children by offering them the best context for their growth and development (AL 205).[40]

Ultimately, this is about approaching young people and making the words with which Pope Francis summarizes the contents of the Gospel of the family relevant to them:

> I would like to say to young people that none of this is jeopardized when their love finds expression in marriage. Their union encounters in this institution the means to ensure that their love truly will endure and grow. Naturally, love is much more than an outward consent or a contract, yet it is nonetheless true that choosing to give marriage a visible form in society by undertaking certain commitments shows how important it is. It manifests the seriousness of each person's identification with the other and their firm decision to leave adolescent individualism behind and to belong to one another. Marriage is a means of expressing that we have truly left the security of the home in which we grew up in order to build other strong ties and to take on a new responsibility for another person. This is much more meaningful than a mere spontaneous association for mutual gratification, which would turn

[40] The reference in AL 2015, note 237, cites: *Relatio* 2014, n. 26; cf. the same words are found, in a more elaborate passage, in: *Relatio* 2015, n. 29.

> marriage into a purely private affair. As a social institution, marriage protects and shapes a shared commitment to deeper growth in love and commitment to one another, for the good of society as a whole. That is why marriage is more than a fleeting fashion; it is of enduring importance. Its essence derives from our human nature and social character. It involves a series of obligations born of love itself, a love so serious and generous that it is ready to face any risk (AL 131; cf. 132).

There are many different paths to follow, but the most important thing is the need to incorporate, as an authentic beacon of light, true love into the specific programs and methodologies of youth ministry, which, strangely enough, have turned their backs on these topics. Nevertheless, as the Holy Father reminds us, these are precisely the issues that interest young people the most. It must not be forgotten that the absence of these topics is due partly to a lack of formation on the part of priests, and of those who facilitate the pastoral care of young people but do not feel sufficiently trained in the matter. Required, then, is the provision of a serious, well-structured plan of formation designed to fill in these gaps.

One of the essential issues that absolutely cannot be omitted is affective-sexual formation. The way in which Pope Francis addresses the subject is enlightening: "Yes to sex education." In this way he evokes the "Nos" that appear in *Evangelii gaudium* (52–75) which he followed up with the corresponding Gospel "Yeses." We must, therefore, say "No" to the trivialization of human sexuality so as not to be robbed of its beauty and grandeur. We must commit ourselves to say "Yes" to affective-sexual education. This is a matter of enormous urgency, particularly given today's trivialization of sexuality (cf. AL 280) and the serious harm this inflicts upon persons. The tragedy is so pronounced, and causes such widespread suffering, that it cannot be ignored, nor can we maintain that ordinary catechetical formation is sufficient. The origins of this situation lie with the loss of the personal meanings of sexuality, following a trend toward mere sensuality.

The urgency of this pastoral imperative is due to the fact

that presently there is a great poverty in this area, which the Pontiff himself deplores: "But who speaks of these things today? Who is capable of taking young people seriously? Who helps them to prepare seriously for a great and generous love? Where sex education is concerned, much is at stake" (AL 284). Every diocese, parish, and Catholic school must respond to these questions, which are so direct that they cannot remain unanswered.

A pastoral experience aware of how prematurely young people in many places engage in sexual relations demands that intervention begin during the pre-adolescent stage. This does not mean organizing some conversation, but rather offering accompaniment that effectively and profoundly touches persons profoundly, so as to help them understand their sexual desire in the light of true love. The Apostolic Exhortation dedicates a full seven paragraphs to such sexual education (AL 280–286), and while this handbook certainly cannot address on the full wealth of reflection offered there, we can point to a few prominent characteristics. A true sexual education does not merely involve giving information, but must also awaken a critical sense with regard to our invasive culture. It must also highlight the importance of modesty and explain the meaning of sexual difference.

We are talking here about invaluable, albeit general, guidelines that must be made concrete within the parameters of specific processes. Promoting them is the task of episcopal conferences and dioceses. Essential to this undertaking is the adoption of a new language that draws upon a certain "language of the body" (AL 284), an expression derived from a source often cited by *Amoris laetitia:* St. Pope John Paul II's catecheses on human love.[41] The first step to take is to make these catecheses known and to

---

[41] See, in particular, AL 151. The Italian edition of John Paul II's catechesis was specially edited by the Pontifical John Paul II Institute for Studies on Marriage and Family. The first published version of the talks with commentary was entitled *Uomo e donna lo creò: Catechesi sull'amore umano* (Rome: Città Nuovo, Libreria Editrice Vaticana, 1985). The authoritative English edition is entitled *Man and Woman He Created Them: A Theology of the Body*, translation and introduction by Michael Waldstein (Boston: Pauline Books & Media, 2006). The Spanish edition prepared by the Pontifical John Paul II Institute is *Hombre y mujer lo creó: El amor humano en el plano divino* (Madrid: Ediciones Cristiandad, 2010).

translate them into a language suitable for young people, as some associations for studying the "Theology of the Body" have done, along with several initiatives organized during World Youth Days, which have taken up this proposal by the "Pope of the family." The success with which these projects have been able to reach young people is effectively demonstrated by their fruitfulness. The task at hand requires a revision of pedagogical methods and a return to the virtues: "The importance of the virtues needs to be included. Among these, chastity proves invaluable for the genuine growth of love between persons" (AL 206, citing *Relatio* 2014, n. 39; cf. *Relatio* 2015, n. 58).

The issues raised by Pope Francis also regard a cultural context that must be taken into consideration when it comes to the pastoral care of young people. A discussion of this context needs to be included among the topics treated by catecheses for these age groups. One must never underestimate the enormous weight that certain ideologies exercise over our youths. In particular, the Apostolic Exhortation warns against the great harm caused by gender ideology, something which Francis himself has cautioned against numerous times, describing it in terms of an "ideological colonization."[42] "It is a source of concern that some ideologies of this sort, which seek to respond to what are at times understandable aspirations, manage to assert themselves as absolute and unquestionable, even dictating how children should be raised" (AL 56).

The clarification of love's true nature in response to its ideological reduction does not replace but rather requires a specific program of sexual education. Such a program cannot be devised in terms of simple conversations, however informative these may be, since this is not how one succeeds in deeply structuring personal behavior. The fundamental meanings of sexuality must come into play. We need to organize such courses in every Catholic school

[42] Cf. Francis, *Address during the Meeting with Families*, January 16, 2015. He insists on this idea: Francis, *General Audience* (April 15, 2015), n. 10: "I ask myself, if the so-called gender theory is not, at the same time, an expression of frustration and resignation, which seeks to cancel out sexual difference because it no longer knows how to confront it. Yes, we risk taking a step backwards. The removal of difference in fact creates a problem, not a solution."

and parish, but must always do so with the collaboration of parents and in a gradual but real, systematic way. At the same time, we need to investigate every possible way of reaching those not receiving a Catholic education.

In order to carry out this education adequately, it is indispensable to have well-trained persons at one's disposal. Otherwise, however good the material may be, every attempt to communicate it well will be unsuccessful. Carefully planned diocesan courses need to be organized for instructing those directly involved in leading the courses. Coordination with an educational pastoral care is also vital, especially with the age groups of twelve- to fourteen-year-olds. It is in this context that programs of help to families that live the experience of having in their midst persons who feel attracted to persons of the same sex, as indicated by the exhortation (cf. AL 250). This is a difficult argument that needs to be made known and promoted by the ordinary pastoral care at the parochial level.

In this context one can also integrate programs aimed at helping families that count among their members persons with same-sex attraction, as the Apostolic Exhortation notes (cf. AL 250). Such programs need to become something that is known and ready at hand in the ordinary pastoral care at the parish level. It is especially urgent properly to form the ecclesial community on this topic, since most Catholics typically know about this issue only from what comes to them through the mass media. Such formation should also result in a proposal for the accompaniment of persons who specifically need it.

b. Accompaniment During the Engagement Period

The second phase of this broader program of marriage preparation occurs during the engagement period itself: "The timely preparation of engaged couples by the parish community should also assist them to recognize eventual problems and risks" (AL 209). Here the term "accompaniment" acquires a special value because, to a large extent, it is a matter of helping persons see love as a profound wisdom capable of confronting the challenges and risks of real life. Instead of seeing time as an enemy of love, it should be regarded as a grace laden path by which God works to mature those who faithfully love each other: "The important thing is to teach [young people] ... sensitivity to different expressions of love, mutual concern and care, loving respect and deeply meaningful communication. All of these prepare them for an integral and generous gift of self that will be expressed, following a public commitment, in the gift of their bodies" (AL 283). The fear of what is perceived as an excessive commitment is due both to the isolation and "privacy" with which young people experience these relations, and to the almost complete absence of any ecclesial mediation that could enlighten them.

A basic requirement, then, at least at the diocesan level, is the need to develop programs that accompany engaged couples. Naturally, this should begin with a pilot preliminary in places where there are already sufficiently trained personnel, as well as engaged couples willing to take such a course. It will be necessary to coordinate efforts across numerous parishes, all within the context of an integral pastoral approach. Assistance from associations of married couples and from youth movements will also be of great value. Should the course be held outside the parish, it would be good to have a parish reception for the fiancées. Concretely, there could be a communal celebration of blessing their commitment. One of the components of this program must be conveying a sense of the spirituality proper to couples (cf. AL 216, 314), so as to help the fiancées understand how God speaks through their love and unites them more deeply than they may think. This is to draw attention to the real meaning of the bond of grace that God himself promises to them.

9. THE SPECIFIC ACCOMPANIMENT OF FAMILIES: THE FIRST YEARS OF MARRIAGE AND THE MATURING OF LOVE

Given the profound, theological manner in which the preceding model of accompaniment has been presented, it is easy to see why it must continue in the first years of marriage: "Both short-term and long-term marriage preparation should ensure that the couple do not view the wedding ceremony as the end of the road" (AL 211). Pastoral accompaniment must be offered to all newlyweds, for as experience shows, the first years of marriage are a critical time for pastoral care. This is central to any pastoral concern for the family and is a topic that received keen interest on the part of the Synods, as well as from *Amoris laetitia* (cf. AL 217–232).

The profound alteration of life together in the family and of the roles of spouses has brought enormous changes to the structure of the family and to its stability. The spouses need to be very creative and invest a lot of effort when it comes to integrating the numerous demands imposed on them today: work, relationships, one's family of origin, and one's in-laws, etc. The sheer number of responsibilities often results in feelings of suffocation and in an isolation from friends, leading ultimately to a veritable anguish whenever these difficulties, which seem utterly to exceed one's capacities, are confronted. Studies show that more than sixty percent of separations occur in the first seven years of marriage. Unless one pays sufficient pastoral attention to this critical phase of married life, one will never be able to keep up with trying to address what ultimately are the grave consequences of pastoral negligence: broken and wounded families that largely find themselves in their difficult situations because they were not cared for at the proper time.

Given the importance of the first years of marriage, the almost total lack of attention paid to young families on the part of our pastoral care is all the more surprising. Undoubtedly, this is partly the result of an antiquated approach to sacramental preparation that views the sacrament as a point of arrival and subsequently leaves the person alone, providing no further points of reference.

Couples in their first years of marriage require similar pastoral attention as priests or religious during the first years of their priestly and religious life, during which many defections occur. The emotive subject finds it quite difficult to embrace a state of life and thus to give shape to his or her future. Assuming stability and being incorporated into a social institution often run counter to people's inmost dispositions. As we have seen (AL 131), Pope Francis specifically takes on this set of problems which is particularly typical of the first years of marriage, during which crisis follows upon crisis. Very often these crises become tragic experiences inasmuch as people confront them superficially and in isolation (cf. AL 41). It is therefore necessary to uphold, as an extremely urgent pastoral principle, the following guideline from *Amoris laetitia*, which cites Part Three of *Familiaris consortio* as its point of reference: "Pastoral accompaniment needs to go beyond the actual celebration of the sacrament" (AL 223). This task is primarily entrusted to parishes and, together with them, "associations, ecclesial movement and new communities" (AL 223).

Given the frailty of people who have barely received a first proclamation of the faith, accompaniment becomes even more urgent when proximate marriage preparation was lacking. It is necessary to review the approach to *immediate* marriage preparation. Its goal must be to highlight the profound relation between the spousal union and the *faith* (something extensively discussed during the Synods, and recognized as extremely important).[43]

Among those who participate in this preparation, aimed directly at the reception of the sacrament, are many couples who have already been living together for several years and who sometimes have children. It would be a serious error to consider these encounters as simply elementary catechesis, without helping couples see how the Church is interested in their lives and offers them, through pastoral accompaniment, the great gift of a new bond brimming with riches. Since no family is an island (cf. AL 33), it is not good for spouses to be alone (cf. Gen 2:18).

Moreover, the way in which this preparation is conducted and offered to those who request marriage should also be reviewed, strengthening, in particular, the way in which the testimony of faith is proposed. One should strive to use all available means to make clear the Church's close proximity to families. The witness

[43] This is discussed in: Francis, *Address to the Tribunal of the Roman Rota*, January 23, 2015; Francis, *Address to the Tribunal of the Roman Rota*, January 22, 2016.

of "experienced" couples (cf. AL 223) who lead their family lives with a missionary disposition that is open to others is crucial for establishing an initial relationship capable of serving as a support. The numerous means of social contact available today help to maintain some kind of relationship, however trivial it may seem. Over the course of this preparation it is also critical that those about to be married know about all the tools the Church places at their disposal to be of help in cases of marital crisis. Only in this way can we overcome the false impressions created by the contemporary idea of "privacy" in which couples believe themselves capable of dealing with these crises on their own. What must likewise be surmounted is the erroneous assumption that the Church limits herself to reminding people of their obligations but does not accompany them, so that she is of no use to anyone in these moments. *Amoris laetitia* contains a clear admonition along these lines: "Marriage preparation should also provide couples with the names of places, people and services to which they can turn for help when problems arise" (AL 211).[44]

Whenever an initial connection is made by way of personal encounter, there is a greater possibility that future accompaniment will be received favorably, without any suspicion of ulterior motives. This is not possible, however, when the presence of an adequate network of couples in the parish is lacking. Often the frustration of spouses who ask the Church to accompany them is real, particularly when they find themselves received by pastors without any interest, who somehow think that such couples are not important enough for ordinary pastoral activity, which is concentrated instead on other aspects.

In connection with this important topic, Pope Francis gives some rather concrete guidelines about what he calls "occasions" for accompaniment:

> I think, for example, of the Baptism and First Holy Communion of their children, or the funerals or weddings of their relatives or friends. Almost all married couples

[44] For the descriptions of these crises cf. AL 232–240.

> reappear on these occasions, and we should take greater advantage of this. Another way of growing closer is by blessing homes or by bringing a pilgrim image of Our Lady to houses in the neighbourhood; this provides an opportunity for a pastoral conversation about the family's situation. It could also be helpful to ask older married couples to help younger couples in the neighbourhood by visiting them and offering guidance in the early years of marriage (AL 230).

The Pope is well aware of the fact that, on this point, we have adopted an inadequate idea of accompaniment. In many cases, the truth is that this has occurred because pastors have followed the youth ministry model, thinking it helpful simply to organize a series of periodic meetings. This offer, however, must seem little attractive for newlywed couples that undergo enormous changes in their lives. Among other factors is the drastic reduction of their free time, especially when their first children are born. *Amoris laetitia* therefore proposes that accompaniment should occur in what are family events by their very nature. Methods may differ considerably based on local practices and customs, but the new approach is to treat these moments as opportunities for accompaniment, counting for this on the right persons, above all experienced couples, who manage to assure the Church's proximate and connatural presence to these families. Above all, one can make the most of those events in which families come together—weddings, Baptisms, First Holy Communions, funerals—to begin a path of accompaniment in their lives. None of this is possible, however, without a significant presence of groups of married people in the parish or in an ecclesial association.

In this sense, those celebrations that require a certain prior catechetical preparation are of particular importance, namely Baptism and First Holy Communion. Experience teaches that on these occasions non-married couples draw near as well. Such persons often desire the benefit of the faith for their children, or at the very least are not averse to it, and experience the occasion as something of a rapprochement with the Church. Thus, when parents who ask for the baptism of their children are welcomed into the parish, it is important to be able to count on the presence of married couples who share this important family event with them. These couples can explain what the birth of a child means for family life; they can give advice on how to go about the very first transmission of the faith and offer accompaniment in the context of a certain friendship. They could even become godparents, if other such suitable persons were lacking. One great advantage of this approach is that it establishes a new relationship that can lead to future encounters. For example, on the second of February, the Feast of the Presentation of our Lord in the Temple, it would be simple to organize a ceremony for all the children baptized in the parish during the previous year. Such an initiative could then be naturally combined with some other sort of occasion, such as a festive meeting or formation session.

Analogously, during the catechetical process of First Holy Communion, one can reach out to the parents, remembering that "family catechesis is of great assistance as an effective method in training young parents to be aware of their mission as the evangelizers of their own family" (AL 287, citing *Relatio* 2015, n. 89). Many relations are established among families who undertake catechesis together, and these can help facilitate a real accompaniment of those weaker in their faith.

Another possibility is to promote other types of family encounters, such as with the custom of blessing homes. It is also promising to form groups of families in the neighborhood, participating in activities that foster significant relationships. One especially recommended method is the celebration of "Parish Family Days," which are simultaneously celebratory, festive, and educational, and often attract large numbers. Also to be considered is the recourse to major demonstrations of popular piety (cf. AL 288, 318), which should be considered as propitious occasions for establishing relationships from which real accompaniment can spring.

What has just been said with respect to marriage preparation and the first years of married life should be understood as "a pedagogy of love, attuned to the feelings and needs of young people and capable of helping them to grow interiorly" (AL 211). All this requires a new model of the family-friendly parish, and beautiful, fruitful examples of this already exist. This is the only way to "renew the covenant between the family and the Christian community" (AL 279).[45]

10. ACCOMPANYING IN FRAILTY: THE DIFFICULT CASES

A special kind of accompaniment is demanded whenever great frailty is found in persons, for one must always be closer to those in need of more help, especially when, like the wounded man in the parable, they cannot travel by themselves. In cases such as these, one must imitate the Good Samaritan and place the person on one's shoulders. This has been a particular concern of Pope Francis from the beginning, and he challenges the Church to develop the response she gives to such persons by way of pastoral accompaniment:

> The Church must accompany with attention and care the weakest of her children, who show signs of a wounded and troubled love, by restoring in them hope and confidence, like the beacon of a lighthouse in a port or a torch carried among the people to enlighten those who have lost their way or who are in the midst of a storm (AL 291, citing *Relatio* 2014, n. 28; cf. *Relatio* 2015, n. 55).

Every case of human frailty must be closely examined if we are to avoid falling into the mistake of unjustly excluding people for sociological reasons. The actual needs and weaknesses of the person must be attended to and not just the striking cases presented by the media. The decisive factor always lies with the difficulty persons have had in facing their Christian life, rather than in the irregularity in which they find themselves, which only ever represents one specific difficulty. Pastorally, initial attention should

[45] Citation: Francis, *Catechesis* (September 9, 2015).

be on addressing and strengthening Christ's intimate presence in the situation of suffering. "Respect needs to be shown especially for the sufferings of those who have unjustly endured separation, divorce or abandonment, or those who have been forced by maltreatment from a husband or a wife to interrupt their life together" (AL 242, citing *Relatio* 2014, n. 47).

The need for a specific kind of pastoral accompaniment is particularly obvious in cases where there is serious need. The Apostolic Exhortation specifically mentions emigration (AL 46), mixed marriages (AL 247), disparity of cult (AL 248), and times of mourning (AL 253–258) as cases that must be treated in a specific way, and here too accompaniment by other couples is highly advisable. A Christian community rich in missionary couples is capable of responding to pastoral needs in even the most sensitive of human realities. Families in such circumstances should never be left alone, or be deprived of guidance or support. Other such special cases include broken marriages, single-parent families, separated persons, and victims of abortion, which are fundamentally the mothers who have aborted.

The Pope specifically highlights the tragedy involved in separations (AL 241), encouraging persons who are not involved in new unions to seek suitable accompaniment (AL 242). We must acknowledge that, generally speaking, it is quite rare to successfully reach this type of person, who experience their tragic breakup in the solitude and sorrow of their families, and not in close contact with their community. Separating according to the canonical norms[46] is quite rare and, consequently, accompaniment is frequently not offered to those going through this exceedingly painful process that affects the whole family community.

Unfortunately, such neglect also widely occurs in cases where the separation has already taken place, and persons are already floundering in isolation. It often happens that such persons do not receive the pastoral attention they so need and want because they are not in an irregular situation. Indeed, even when we speak of difficult situations, the case of separated individuals is scarcely

[46] Cf. *Codex Iuris Canonici* (1983), canons 1152–1155.

mentioned, and one gets the impression that much more attention is given to those who have contracted a new union.

It would of course be Pharisaical to spend a significant amount of time on irregular situations while marginalizing separated persons, as though we could simply be content with congratulating them on being faithful to their marital bond. To do so would be tantamount to adopting a small-minded legalism insensitive to the real and profound sufferings that the person is undergoing. One must pay careful attention to this problem that requires assistance, understanding, and guidance very close to the person and his or her situation.

Associations of families, if well organized, can welcome separated persons without them feeling strange or judged, and can offer a community in which they can become actively integrated. The resources provided by such associations are vital for this kind of pastoral accompaniment. The ecclesial community recognizes that separated persons "often bear witness to marital fidelity" (AL 242, citing *Relatio* 2014, n. 50; cf. *Relatio* 2015, n. 83). Existing associations of separated persons remaining faithful to their marriage bond are a fine example.

All this is even more important when considering the primary victims of separation: children. Children frequently experience separation as a severe trauma, one with numerous consequences. However, despite this, they often do not receive adequate help from the Church. Pope Francis takes utmost interest in emphasizing this point, as is clear in the way he addresses those who have separated: "I make this appeal to parents who are separated: 'Never ever take your child hostage!'" (AL 245).[47] The same plea appears later in reference to the healing of wounds inflicted on children: "[The Church] cannot fail to speak out on behalf of those who are most vulnerable: the children who often suffer in silence" (AL 246). This specific aspect of pastoral care must be a part of Family Counseling Centers and should be appropriately integrated in parish and school programs as well.

---

[47] Citing: Francis, *Catechesis* (May 20, 2015): *L'Osservatore Romano*, English edition, May 21, 2015, p. 8.

In dealing with single-parent families, the Church must act as a true mother (AL 252, *Relatio* 2015, n. 80). Sometimes this can begin as early as the pregnancy itself, accompanying the mother in this difficulty (cf. AL 197). By addressing the mother's practical needs and recognizing her dignity both as a mother and as an educator of her children, the Church's attention will be tactful and compassionate. Although recourse to social assistance programs will always be necessary in such cases, accompaniment can never be simply reduced to this. The closeness of other families will also be of great assistance for the single parent and the children.

Special assistance must be provided for persons who have had an abortion to help them overcome the serious conflict in which they find themselves. They have in fact become victims of the very sin they have committed. In many cases they will need help to overcome the post-abortion syndrome, with all that this involves psychologically, personally, spiritually, and from the perspective of human relationships. No diocesan pastoral plan can fail to offer assistance programs along these lines. Even though this is not mentioned in *Amoris laetitia*, it is nevertheless part of the internal logic of a pastoral accompaniment aimed at addressing the person's fragility as desired by the papal exhortation.

11. "IRREGULAR" CASES

Amoris laetitia returns to the terminology of "irregular" cases that the Synods sought to avoid. We understand "irregular" cases to be situations that contradict the Church's canonical rules, as determined by clear, objective criteria and with consequences in the legal sphere as well. Due to the seriousness of any incident that concerns the juridical sphere of justice, these cases call for special accompaniment and require the adoption of particular measures, especially when dealing with persons who have no intention of ending an unjust situation that has become habitual.

The Apostolic Exhortation reiterates the Synod's directive: "Priests have the duty to 'accompany [divorced and remarried persons] in helping them to understand their situation according to the teaching of the Church and the guidelines of the bishop'" (AL 300). The teaching of the Church and the guidelines of the bishop need to be our point of departure. On account of the enormous scope of the problem, the papal document is necessarily generic, and argues primarily at the level of general principles, all without claiming to descend into the concrete details of the many different situations that can arise. In our text we will present a model for applying these principles concretely, based on experiences gained in various localities.

We will begin with a prudential consideration. Experience has shown that setting up well-defined procedures (at least at the diocesan level) with professionally trained persons who are specifically equipped to work in such situations (i.e., priests, consecrated religious, couples, etc.) is of great advantage. Doing so supplies harmony, establishes common criteria, and avoids waste and ambiguity in how such accompaniment is to be understood. The explicit references in *Amoris laetitia* to the possible risks of arbitrariness, in which priests autonomously grant exceptions (AL 300), and rigidity, in which pastors only apply general rules (AL 2), tend to corroborate this approach as the correct one. The guidelines concerning the need for "specialized counselling centres in dioceses" for pastoral care, which involve "efforts at reconciliation and mediation" (AL 242, citing *Relatio* 2014, n. 47; cf. *Relatio* 2015, n. 79), resemble the procedures described by the Motu proprio, *Mitis Iudex,* which speaks of forming a "stable structure" to assist in cases of nullity.[48] These initiatives support the authorized intervention of bishops because they centralize the pastoral attention given to these cases. This, then, is the response to the requests made by the Synods.[49] No priest

[48] Cf. Francis, Motu proprio, *Mitis Iudex Dominus Iesus* (August 15, 2015), "The way of proceeding in cases regarding the declaration of the nullity of a marriage," art. 3.

[49] Cf. *Relatio* 2014, n. 52: "Access to the sacraments might take place if preceded by a penitential practice, determined by the diocesan bishop"; *Relatio* 2015, n. 53: "Hopefully, dioceses will promote various means of discernment for these people and to involve them in the community to help and encourage them to grow and eventually make a conscious, coherent choice."

may independently claim the authority to conduct his own personal process. Pastors must always invite persons in these situations to comply with diocesan procedures. Such measures, on the one hand, are supportive of priests, who feel simultaneously accompanied and protected by their bishop in cases where potentially groundless claims are presented, and, on the other hand, are profound guarantors of the experience of ecclesial communion, which is especially important in matters connected with the family.

To assign the ecclesial discernment of "difficult cases" to specific diocesan programs or pastoral regions is an act of prudence. Such programs allow everyone to be accompanied as cases are adjudicated individually. Whenever such procedures are put in place, persons are taken seriously and one avoids the impression of arbitrariness, or of hasty, emotional solutions devoid of well-founded reasoning. This is the way to act according to "the teaching of the Church," as required by the Apostolic Exhortation, which in turn takes up the requests made by the Synod (AL 300).

Everything just mentioned must be done in a manner coordinated with pastoral care as a whole. In other words, initial accompaniment should be carried out in parishes, which will then have its ramifications at the diocesan level. In this way people will not be removed from their communities of reference, which is where the process of integration, as will soon be discussed, takes place. At the same time they receive the attention appropriate for their situation.

12. THE INTERNAL FORUM

The very mention of the internal forum, as it appears in the Apostolic Exhortation, clarifies for the reader the proper understanding of this rapport: "Conversation with the priest, in the internal forum, contributes to the formation of a correct judgment on what hinders the possibility of a fuller participation in the life of the Church and on what steps can foster it and make it grow" (AL 300, citing *Relatio* 2015, n. 85). Such help is always part of a broader process, since any solution of the internal forum is not enough to resolve the question of admission to the sacraments when Catholics are living in a situation of manifest grave sin. This principle has already been explained by the Pontifical Council for the Interpretation of Legislative Texts in its Declaration dated June 24, 2000, which is precisely one of the sources employed by the Apostolic Exhortation (AL 302, note 345).[50]

Intervention in the internal forum, although it is a particularly appropriate method of accompaniment, must be complemented by other pastoral elements in the external forum, such as those presented by *Amoris laetitia*. In particular, it is easy to show how a person would refer to a priest concrete matters of conscience that belong to the internal forum, such as those relating to the personal fulfillment of the requirements necessary to receiving the sacraments. Ultimately, the interpretation of the process in the internal forum must be understood according to the explanation given by Joseph Ratzinger in his capacity as Prefect of the Congregation for the Doctrine of the Faith.[51] On the basis of this authoritative analysis and interpretation, the practice of the internal forum must be understood as follows: It is the help that these persons need in order to come to accept the requirement to live "in full continence."[52] This is of course something only to be confirmed in the internal forum in a pastorally sensitive manner while remaining

---

[50] It was also already cited in a similar way by *Relatio* 2015, n. 85.

[51] Congregation for the Doctrine of the Faith, *Letter to the Bishops of the Catholic Church Concerning the Reception of Holy Communion by the Divorced and Remarried Members of the Faithful* (September 14, 1994).

[52] The document is meant to clarify the "Note" from the Congregation for the Doctrine of the Faith dated April 11, 1973, and the letter from its Secretary, Archbishop Hamer, dated March 21, 1975. Cf. also Joseph Ratzinger, "Introduzione," in: Congregazione per la Dottrina della Fede, *Sulla pastorale dei divorziati risposati* (Città del Vaticano: Libreria Editrice Vaticana, 1998), 18–19: "This means concretely that they should repent of having broken the sacramental matrimonial bond . . . if they separate from the person who is not their legitimate spouse. If this is not possible for serious reasons, for example the education of the children, they must resolve to live in complete continence (cf. FC 84). With the help of grace that overcomes everything . . . it must be transformed more and more into a bond of friendship, respect, and mutual aid. This is the interpretation that *Familiaris consortio* gives of the so-called 'approved practice of the Church in the internal forum.'" [Translated from Italian.]

within the context of a broader process of accompaniment by the ecclesial community under the direction of the bishop.[53]

It is logical for the bishop to appoint some priests particularly well-trained for this accompaniment in the internal forum within the context of the assistance offered by the itinerary that we are outlining. All this must never exclude the counsel of other well-trained priests, particularly those closest to these individuals, who have initially accompanied them and encouraged them to follow the aforesaid process.

13. THREE STEPS ALONG A PATH

We will now proceed to briefly explain the three parts that must structure accompaniment in order for it to be an itinerary of personal growth with different steps. Time is essential, as is the dialogue that occurs along the way. It is the task of the bishop to establish the steps to be taken, so as to help persons clarify their situation. This is one way of presenting the Church as a Mother who offers a path of maturation to these persons.

In accordance with the desire of Pope Francis, who expresses this at the conclusion of his thoughts on "irregular" situations, every itinerary or program must be adapted to the specific situations in which people find themselves.

> I encourage the faithful who find themselves in complicated situations to speak confidently with their pastors or with other lay people whose lives are committed to the Lord. They may not always encounter in them a confirmation of their own ideas or desires, but they will surely receive some light to help them better understand their situation and discover a path to personal growth. I also encourage the Church's pastors to listen to them with

[53] Cf. Joseph Ratzinger, "Introduzione," p. 19: "It is clear to everyone that this solution is demanding, especially if the persons in question are young. For this reason the wise, fatherly accompaniment of a confessor is of particularly great importance." [Translated from Italian.]

> sensitivity and serenity, with a sincere desire to understand their plight and their point of view, in order to help them live better lives and to recognize their proper place in the Church (AL 312).

Of course, the way in which this path is offered must never give the impression of permissiveness with regard to irregularities; otherwise the result will be a gradualness of the law. It is also not a matter of offering exceptional solutions to problems, since this could only be understood from the perspective of a kind of legalism. This would be the equivalent of saying that the law is too difficult, and that the only way forward is to find exceptions to the rules. By contrast, the right attitude is one that communicates the need for a time of maturation in the faith, during which the accompaniment of the community is also made available. Although the process we are presenting here is designed specifically for divorced persons who have civilly remarried, it could, with appropriate modifications, also prove to be useful in cases of cohabiting couples or civilly married persons (cf. AL 293 and 78), who must also be accompanied, and whose situations usually are less complex.

a. Welcoming Persons

The initial step of pastoral accompaniment is always to welcome the persons and never consider them as "one of many cases." Such a welcoming must be situated within a framework of integration, which we will describe in greater detail in the next chapter. Welcoming also has a decisively evangelical character, which is different from the approach of a society that supposes it can completely resolve marital problems by breaking up the marriage, as though one could simply begin all over again. Although such an approach may, at first, seem attractive, it is in fact the farthest thing imaginable from genuine accompaniment on account of the false concept of freedom upon which it relies: "Relationships are left to the changing winds of personal desire and circumstances" (AL 34). The individual is not a problem to be solved or a case to be settled, and the Church possesses both human and divine wisdom that enables her to genuinely attend to persons and their needs.

Ordinary pastoral care offers countless opportunities for drawing closer to divorced or cohabiting persons. It is, for example, a common experience that it is possible to reach out to parents through their children, and we have already spoken of some occasions on which this could occur, that is, when couples request Baptism for their children; when they ask for the First Communion catechesis; when they seek help for their children with learning difficulties in school. Such requests by the divorced and civilly remarried or cohabiting parents are much more common than their demands to receive the sacraments. The Church meets and receives them as Christian believers. All these opportunities allow pastors to welcome parents tactfully, while still making them aware of their situation and of their responsibility toward their children. For such rapprochement to be realized with great sensitivity, the cooperation of families in these areas of pastoral care is also critically important.

The initial welcome is to be carried out within the ecclesial community, typically a parish, by way of a timely invitation to participate and be acquainted with parish life. In this way, persons will view the Church not as some kind of service organization, but as a place of family life. Parents are thus given an initial affective sense of belonging to the Church, and this is the first step in a process of vital integration and growth in the Church.

True welcoming is the foundation for an initial accompaniment in which the couple will want to *examine the truth of their situation*. This examination will help them come to appreciate the differences among various situations (AL 298). It may also give rise to difficulties when the partners are of divergent opinions or when the examination regards previous unions. It is crucial to recall that welcoming means beginning a journey and not accepting things as they are, as if the welcoming itself already implied the right to receive the sacraments. The purpose is not immediately to resolve a problem but to establish a relationship by which an itinerary may be offered. Gradual, affective integration into the community is of great help along these lines. The setting in which the family lives is also necessarily involved in this initial act of acquaintance, particularly with respect to children, and this includes those from previous unions. What has already been said in reference to separated persons applies here as well.

Only once the welcome is concluded, and a certain degree of stability in dialogue and accompaniment has been reached, can the pastor form an initial judgment about the situation. This must not be a judgment concentrated solely on potential irregularities, but must also consider the frailty and wounds of the person, as well as the difficulties they may face in realizing the true love proclaimed by the Gospel. It is on the basis of this initial judgment that persons should be directed to diocesan programs focused on further phases of accompaniment, and this will be discussed in the following paragraphs. But these can be very complex situations, and may require a considerable time before it is possible to address their difficulties in depth. In the case of couples who live life far from faith, it is first necessary to invite these persons to individual formation, which is indispensable if they are to have an elementary knowledge of marriage and the family according to the Gospel.

During first contact, more or less obvious signs of the possible nullity of the preceding marriage may emerge. Even the annulment process presents an excellent opportunity for pastoral accompaniment so that those concerned understand better the Church's way of proceeding in these matters.

The guideline of the Motu proprio *Mitis Iudex* (cf. AL 244), on the expediency of a "stable structure" at the diocesan and inter-diocesan levels,[54] can be incorporated into what has already been proposed with respect to the centralized structure of pastoral accompaniment programs.[55] The Tribunal of the Roman Rota, in explaining the application of this Decree, specifies that its function must be "a service of information, of counselling and of mediation, attached to the office of the family pastoral

---

[54] Francis, *Mitis Iudex*, "The way of proceeding...," art. 3.

[55] This would be developed "within the unified diocesan pastoral care of marriage," as described in the Motu proprio (cf. Francis, *Mitis Iudex*, "The way of proceeding...," art. 2).

service."[56] Since this service includes an element of mediation, "*This path of 'accompanying' will aid in overcoming* in a more satisfying manner matrimonial crises, but it is also called to verify, in concrete cases, the validity or non-validity of the marriage."[57]

b. A Proposal for a Faith Itinerary Composed of Several Levels

The second step of a pastoral program of accompaniment is related to the importance of faith for Christian conversion. This is a matter of proclaiming to these divorced persons the truth of the Gospel as a light for their lives, according to a method adapted to their concrete situations, so that they can interpret their stories not as a dead end but in terms of God's proximity, which opens up a path of salvation.

The model to follow will be that of a new Christian initiation, to which the faithful have access as persons already baptized. It is necessary to propose this path on two levels. The first is more general: their participation in an adult catechumenate, as part of their incorporation into the community, aimed at helping them understand the fundamental elements of the Christian life. The second level is more specific and concerns the details of their situation relative to the Gospel of marriage and the family. Those responsible for conducting this initiation must receive specific training in these matters. The most suitable solution would be to have a group of qualified priests and married couples who can visibly witness to the Church's presence.

The first stage of this proposal is obviously addressed at persons who, having little knowledge of the faith, need to hear the good news of Christianity in their first welcome: "The Gospel message and its call to conversion" (AL 297) must be offered to them. As to content, the adult formation program will begin with presenting the vital significance of Baptism, by which the faithful

---

[56] Apostolic Tribunal of the Roman Rota, *Subsidium for the Application of the Motu Proprio Mitis Iudex Dominus Iesus* (Vatican City, January 2016), I, 1.

[57] Ibid.

are incorporated into the Church. It will then proceed to faith formation. Faith touches the totality of one's existence and must be lived out in its entirety. Note the correspondence to Christian initiation: a maturation of faith that prepares one to participate fully in the life of the Church. It is, therefore, fundamentally important to present the main lines of God's plan of salvation: The mystery of God's love is manifested and accomplished in Jesus Christ who has given us his Holy Spirit, so that we might live in covenant with him. This covenant realizes God's unconditional and unfailing spousal love for his Church, a love that conquers sin and death. It is the gift of this love that we receive in the sacraments and to which we must give witness in our actions and in our praise of God.

The way in which the Gospel is presented must illuminate and influence the everyday events of life. It is particularly important to examine complex concepts such as divine revelation, God's covenant with humankind, and the mystery of Trinitarian Communion, all without forgetting the relation between Christ's redemption, the mystery of the Church, and the truth of the sacraments. Only then does it become possible to contextualize the Christian understanding of the Sacrament of Matrimony and its fundamental characteristics.

The second level of the faith itinerary proposed here aims at understanding the indissoluble marriage bond as an expression of being "one flesh" (cf. Gen 2:24). In this way one can comprehend the exclusive character of the act of giving oneself in the body. Indeed, one can speak of a "co-ownership of the bodies," since "the wife does not rule over her own body, but the husband does; likewise the husband does not rule over his own body, but the wife does" (1 Cor 7:4).

In other words, the purpose of this phase is to present fundamental criteria necessary for the discernment of the concrete situation and of the path to travel—also in view of overcoming sin. In this way, non-married couples will know the truth of what the Church teaches about marriage and the reasons upon which her pastoral practice is based. In this way, these couples will be better able to understand that God's mercy can heal the infidelity that has given rise to their situation; they will appreciate that this mercy can heal the resulting wounds and offences and that it can open a path of true conversion. Close, loving pastoral care is thus capable of bringing about what *Amoris laetitia* calls "the awareness of their situation before God" (AL 300, citing *Relatio* 2015, n. 86).

This stage could likewise include several *ritual transitions* that run parallel to the rite of Christian initiation of adults. By doing so, one could promote greater personal commitment, while always keeping in sight the total conversion to Christ. Visible signs are important for reinforcing a sense of community, and it is never helpful to think of Eucharistic communion as the only sign of belonging. In any case, these signs must be administered individually and privately, so that there is not the slightest suggestion of blessing the couple, which would contradict the intrinsic logic of the whole process.

Since this itinerary is a process of ecclesial integration, an appropriate value must be assigned to the participation of the community in this rite of adult initiation. In this way, one assures that the rite's meaning is to lead to conversion. A vivid example of such kind of itinerary is offered by the Neocatechumenal communities, which welcome many divorced persons and bring about a significant number of conversions by introducing them to their path. Friendship and fellowship with other couples is a privileged way of gradually overcoming the many circumstances that obstruct such a process of conversion.

c. A Path of Conversion in the Perspective of the Possible Reception of the Sacraments

The third step is one that Jesus took with the Samaritan woman: By confronting her with the truth of her story, he enabled her to see the obstacles that continued to arise in her life in opposition to the demands of following him. Accepting this principle means being aware that following Christ involves changing one's way of life. The catechesis that the persons in question have previously received will have clarified this fact for them. It is therefore possible to present this as a step along the path of conversion, provided that a suitable ecclesial accompaniment is offered.

This step begins when some of these persons ask to set out on a special path of conversion with the perspective of receiving the Sacraments of Penance and the Eucharist under the proper conditions. Let us recall that it is the individual who is admitted to the sacraments, even as it is still preferable that the couple be committed to following this path together, for each could then support the other in tackling these various stages. From the outset, the partners must be aware of the demands implied in each step, given that the discernment involved is ecclesial and not merely subjective.

At this point it is crucial that accompaniment be offered in accordance with the specific way in which each person lives out the faith and progressively complies with the requirements of the Gospel. The personalization of the path is critically important, and one must therefore know how to deal with the specific questions of *each person,* which may be different for each member of the couple.

The whole process of formation hinges on the matter of forgiveness. First of all, one has to be clear about its object. *What needs forgiveness is not only the rupture of the previous marriage. One also needs to discern the real existence of the preceding marital bond and consider the fact that uniting oneself sexually to a person other than one's spouse means committing the sin of adultery.* Christian forgiveness is born from the grace of eternal mercy.

From this love, which reaches the heart, a disposition to be reconciled with one's spouse—from whom one has separated—needs to be formed. Likewise, the desire to repair the injustices proper to any rupture needs to be nurtured, while being conscious of the fact that "to forgive such an injustice that has been suffered is not easy, but grace makes this journey possible" (AL 242, citing *Relatio* 2014, n. 47; cf. *Relatio* 2015, n. 79).

Beginning with the logic of forgiveness that accompanies this whole phase, we can propose a series of steps aimed at clarifying the truth of the situation with respect to the sacramental reality of the couple:

- the recognition that they have acted contrary to the Gospel of Christ in a matter that is crucial for their lives and vocation, and for the building up of society and the Church;
- the recognition that by being unfaithful to their marital promise, they have failed with respect to the exclusivity that is proper to true love;
- the recognition that they have inflicted harm and pain to their previous families and, in particular, to the spouse and to the children born of the sacramental bond;
- the recognition of the scandal caused to other persons, particularly young people;
- the disposition to repair the harm done to the degree that this is possible;
- the request for forgiveness from their one and only true spouse;
- the recognition of the first bond's divine and sacramental permanence;
- the firm resolve to live in accordance with the truth of said bond, and to remain attendant to the Gospel in their present situation.

By living in a manner consistent with the truth of an existing previous bond, whether by abandoning the new union or, if this is not possible, practicing continence within it, the partners can be admitted to the Sacrament of Reconciliation and to the Eucharist, as long as adequate care is being taken to avoid scandal.[58] Here, then, is a concrete, evangelical, and real way of bringing to a conclusion what *Amoris laetitia* proposes: "an examination of conscience through moments of reflection and repentance" (AL 300, citing *Relatio* 2015, n. 85).[59]

---

[58] Cf. John Paul II, *Familiaris consortio*, n. 84.

[59] *Amoris laetitia* presents the following aspects as points for reflection: "[H]ow did they act towards their children when the conjugal union entered into crisis; whether or not they made attempts at reconciliation; what has become of the abandoned party; what consequences the new relationship has on the rest of the family and the community of the faithful; and what example is being set for

There is clearly a need to offer support along a path that at any rate remains difficult. It will help to have experienced the goodness of accompaniment in a broad process in which the partners are sustained in forming a new affectivity and a different mode of acting. The whole previous itinerary will thus have prepared them for this final step, above all by forming the virtue of chastity, which is now adapted to the new situation.

With the admission to the sacraments the process of accompaniment does not come to an end. Rather, now a path can begin. The Church's presence is particularly necessary on account of the difficulties that will arise as these persons strive to remain faithful to their resolution.[60]

young people who are preparing for marriage." All of these are summarized and incorporated into our proposal.

[60] This is said, specifically, in relation to what is involved in living as brother and sister, cf. AL 298, note 329. This also refers implicitly to what John Paul II declares in *Familiaris consortio*, n. 84: "they take on themselves the duty to live in complete continence, that is, by abstinence from the acts proper to married couples."

CHAPTER TWO

Integrating: The Return to Full Communion

ACCOMPANYING, discerning, integrating. We have seen the urgency of accompaniment, through which the Church becomes close to a person whose love is wounded and troubled (AL 291) because it revolves around itself: "one's personality is shaped by his or her desires, which are considered absolute" (AL 33). The Church offers to all human beings the space of her communion, which saves them from the postmodern deluge of fluid loves, as a new Noah's ark that rescues the human family. Hope can be revived only by experiencing this concrete presence that comes about when a brother or sister is welcomed: it is possible for everyone to live the great life that Jesus promises.

Once it has illustrated the concept of "accompaniment," *Amoris laetitia* speaks about "discernment" and "integration." So as to reflect the internal logic of the process more accurately, in this manual we will invert the proposed order: we will seek first to understand what "integration" means—in other words, what the ultimate goal of the path of accompaniment is. Indeed, one can discern only if one has clearly in mind the final point toward which the path leads: what is discerned or verified, in reality, is not the final goal but rather the best way to follow in order to arrive at it. St. Ignatius of Loyola knew this quite well; in his *Spiritual Exercises* he puts in the very first place his meditation on "First Principle and Foundation," a consideration of the end for which man was created.[1]

Where does *Amoris laetitia*, for its part, ask us to guide loves that are wounded and troubled (AL 291)?

1. THE GOAL OF THE PATH: INTEGRATING INTO THE FULL LIFE OF CHRIST

Amoris laetitia proposes a way to follow in order to incorporate fully into the Church those who have fallen away from a life in keeping with the Gospel and are living in "irregular" situations, that is to say, families that are suffering because of a "troubled love" (cf. AL 291): those who are cohabiting, civil marriages, divorced and "remarried" persons. . . . This full incorporation into the Church involves, according to Pope Francis, the development of the "fullness of God's plan for them" (AL 297), that is, the vocation to marriage as a call that comes from God. In the case of the divorced it is a question, therefore, of living in a way that remains faithful to the sacramental bond that they have contracted, by which the Lord united their life to that of their true spouse. *Amoris laetitia* recalls several times that it is not possible to abandon this goal: the goodness of every step of the accompaniment is measured by whether it draws closer to or leads away from the ultimate goal (cf. AL 293–294; 297; 307; 325).[2] We note *the harmony between this perspective and Amoris laetitia as a whole, which*

---

[1] Cf. *The Spiritual Exercises of St. Ignatius: A New Translation* by Louis J. Puhl, S.J. (Westminster, MD: The Newman Press, 1959).

[2] Cf. AL 293: it is up to the pastors "to distinguish elements in their lives that can lead to a greater openness to the Gospel of marriage in its fullness"; Al 294: "opportunities that can lead to the full reality of marriage and family"; AL 297: "offering them assistance so they can reach the fullness of God's plan for them"; AL 307: "in no way must the Church desist from proposing the full ideal of marriage"; AL 325: "never . . . stop seeking that fullness of love."

asks us to develop a "pastoral care centred on the bond"[3] as well as "a spirituality of the bond."[4] This bond is conjugal love, unique and indivisible, the love that God himself established (cf. Mt 19:6). Pastoral care centered on the bond unifies marital pastoral care: it prepares young people so that they might be able to pronounce their "Yes" forever; it helps them to grow during the first years of family life; it accompanies spouses who are going through difficulties.

Therefore *pastoral care centered on the bond must also be the care suited to divorced persons who have remarried civilly*: it is about helping to bring them back to the matrimonial bond that the Lord had given them, and to live in keeping with that bond. Even though union with the spouse cannot be reestablished in some cases, it is better not to speak about irreversible situations: the decision to live in a way contrary to the conjugal bond is, in fact, always reversible. This possibility was already included from the beginning in the matrimonial promise in which, with the help of Jesus, they said "Yes" to each other for ever and "in spite of everything" (cf. AL 118). The grace itself of the Sacrament of Matrimony operates along these lines, inviting spouses to build on the foundations that God himself has laid, the only ones that can keep the house standing. Indeed, as Pope Francis points out, "Their union is real and irrevocable, confirmed and consecrated by the sacrament of matrimony" (AL 218).

The parable of the prodigal son tells us about this process, presenting it as integration into his father's household: "And he arose and returned to his father's house. But while he was yet at a distance, his father saw him and had compassion, and ran to meet him and embraced him and kissed him" (cf. Lk 15:20). This is a path of conversion and regeneration of heart, a path toward which God himself urges us, while he comes to meet us, to welcome his son who is returning. In the embrace we can see an allusion to the Sacrament of Reconciliation. Right afterward the father says:

---

[3] AL 211: "The pastoral care of engaged and married couples should be centred on the marriage bond."

[4] AL 315: "In the end, marital spirituality is a spirituality of the bond, in which divine love dwells."

"Bring quickly the best robe, and put it on him; and put a ring on his hand, and shoes on his feet; and bring the fatted calf and kill it; and let us eat and make merry" (cf. Lk 15:22–24). According to the Fathers of the Church, the ring and the robe symbolize the dignity of the son and of the spouse. This is a return to a life according to his baptismal and matrimonial promises, a life that the baptized person can now begin anew. Finally, as the climax of the path, the Lamb is sacrificed and the household participates in the Eucharistic banquet.

2. INCOMPLETE PARTICIPATION AND A PATH OF INTEGRATION

We may wonder: why are special efforts necessary to integrate these baptized persons? Are they not already in the Church? In reference to divorced persons in a new union, *Amoris laetitia* reminds us, in fact, that "they belong to the Church as the body of Christ": "they are baptized; they are brothers and sisters" (AL 299). And so it is: through Baptism they were incorporated in Christ; imprinted on them they have the seal of Jesus that continually calls them to live according to the Gospel. Furthermore, there is no canonical excommunication imposed on these baptized persons that would prevent them from taking part in the ongoing life of the Church: attending the liturgy, collaborating in her works of charity and in the mission of evangelization. . . . Indeed, they have the obligation to educate their children in the faith, a mission for which God will not deny them his grace.

Nevertheless, this participation in the Church is not complete. What is lacking?

It is necessary to recall that one does not belong to the Church merely through an invisible connection: this would be the Protestant view, instead. No doubt, for full incorporation it is necessary to possess the Holy Spirit who dwells in the hearts of the faithful. Nevertheless, there are also criteria of visible incorporation, because the Church is a community that springs from the Incarnation and concerns the whole person, not just his soul, but also his body. Only in this way does the Church transform the world in which we live, suffer, work, and love. A merely invisible Church would be, in the final analysis, an individualistic Church, in which each person would relate alone to his own God. In the Catholic Church, in contrast, salvation reaches souls through concrete relationships that offer themselves to us in the body and bind us to God and to our brethren. This is why the Church is called "the *Body* of Christ" and "the universal *sacrament* of salvation."[5]

There are three main criteria for visible membership:[6] professing and living out the faith of the Church; being in communion with the body of the Church, through her pastors; and leading a life that is in harmony with the sacraments. The last point is precisely the one where the main difficulty appears in dealing with these Catholics: the lack of consistency with the sacramental life which, in turn, influences the first aspect, the life of faith. The fact is that these persons have chosen to build their concrete, visible relationships in a way contrary to the Gospel and to the logic of the sacraments. In doing so, they broke their baptismal and matrimonial promises and violated the dynamism of the Eucharist, which contains the spousal love of Christ for his Church. This is why these Catholics have a journey to make before attaining full participation in the life of the Church.

These three criteria for membership fit together harmoniously in charity, according to the *via caritatis* mentioned in AL 306. Professing the faith—the first criterion—means confessing the fullness of this love, as it is lived and taught by Jesus in the Gospel (including his teaching on marriage). Someone who lives in love lives also in communion with his brethren through their pastors—the second criterion; this communion reflects the spousal love of the Head and of the body, of Christ and of the Church. Finally—the third criterion—living in love means accepting in the flesh Jesus' way of living, as transmitted to us by the sacraments. In other words, it is a matter of living according to the charity about which St. Paul says, in his second hymn to love: "Owe no

[5] Second Vatican Council, *Lumen gentium*, n. 48.

[6] Cf. Acts 2:42; Second Vatican Council, *Lumen gentium*, n. 14.

one anything, except to love one another; for he who loves his neighbor has fulfilled the law. The commandments, 'You shall not commit adultery, You shall not kill, You shall not steal, You shall not covet,' and any other commandment, are summed up in this sentence, 'You shall love your neighbor as yourself.' Love does no wrong to a neighbor; therefore love is the fulfilling of the law" (Rom 13:8–10). We can therefore declare that "love covers a multitude of sins" (1 Pet 4:8, cited in AL 306[7]) since it leads us to full communion, as opposed to isolation and estrangement from God, that is to say, sin. The participation of persons in the charitable works of the Church, or the dimension of ecclesial *diakonia*,[8] is certainly one way of journeying toward integration into the Church; nevertheless, in light of this, it is necessary to understand that full communion can be attained only in the Eucharist, the source of all charity.

It is necessary to be cautious so as not to confuse the integration that *Amoris laetitia* speaks about, which consists of taking part in a mystery of communion, with mere social inclusion. In the latter case it is a matter of eliminating the obstacles that have been set up illegitimately through injustice or iniquity. According to this logic, a marginalized person is someone whose fundamental rights are not respected, someone who is being discriminated against. Integration consists of reforming structures or norms that are external to the person, so that he or she may be considered equal to everyone else. Logically, it is necessary to avoid any attitude of this sort in dealing with any Catholic (cf. AL 296). Nevertheless, the logic of full participation in the Church is different, since it consists in being a member not only of a society of individuals with equal rights, but also of a communion in which life itself is shared by accepting a gift that originates with God. The one who does not participate fully is someone who is not open to this gift. It is necessary therefore to begin a process of interior transformation

[7] In the same paragraph the document cites Dan 4:24: "Atone for your sins with righteousness, and your iniquities with mercy to the oppressed, so that your prosperity may be prolonged"; Sir 3:30: "As water extinguishes a blazing fire, so almsgiving atones for sins."

[8] Cf. Benedict XVI, *Deus Caritas Est*, n. 25.

of the person so that he or she might participate in the life that Christ bestows and might be conformed to it.

3. HEALING THE WOUNDS THAT PREVENT FULL PARTICIPATION

Like a good physician, we too must inquire about the nature of the wound that has caused this lack of full membership in the Church. The process of integration will be aimed specifically at healing the wound in question.

The first point to keep in mind is the following: *the cause of this absence of membership is not the failure of the first marriage.* Its breakup, certainly, was very painful and caused serious wounds, and it will take patience to heal them (cf. AL 241–242). Nevertheless, this does not necessarily mean that there was any personal guilt, which is the most serious wound, since it refers to the person's relationship with God. This is clear, for example, in the case of the spouse who is unjustly abandoned, the innocent victim of the breakup. The failure of one's marriage, in itself, does not put a person in an ongoing situation that contradicts Christ's words (cf. Mt 19:9; Mt 5:31; Mk 10:11–12; Lk 16:18; 1 Cor 7:10–11). Indeed, *Amoris laetitia* 242 says that "divorced persons who have not remarried . . . often bear witness to marital fidelity."

What, then, is the real malady that afflicts these persons? It is the second union that they have contracted. This is the cause of their illness, since this act that they have committed and the resulting state in which they find themselves is what puts them in contradiction to Christ's words. In establishing the second union, they intended to bury their matrimonial bond, building their life apart from the foundation that God had laid. In doing so, they denied the truth of the promise, guaranteed by Jesus, of a love that is "forever" and "in spite of everything." As long as they live in contradiction to the matrimonial bond, their life will be fragmented, since it will be led in terms of a "second or third chance." (If it was possible to build a new life by breaking that promise then, as a matter of principle, it will be possible to build still others by breaking later promises). Consequently, they will have great difficulty transmitting to their children something that is essential for their education: confidence that it is possible to build a whole life on true love, entrusting our whole future to it.

In discussing the topic of accompaniment, we already saw how the Church must be moved with mercy in view of this suffering and must help persons in a concrete way to get out of it. From what has been said, it is clear how difficult a wound this is to heal, since often the persons do not realize its importance, are afraid to acknowledge it, and justify their second union. This is why it will be a delicate, patient task, which must rely on God's light and grace, in order to help our brothers and sisters to leave the house built on sand and to establish themselves once again on the rock on which they can build with hope (cf. AL 8).

In this connection we need to avoid any ambiguity with respect to mercy. In fact, nowadays *mercy sometimes tends to be equated with an emotional sort of compassion that bends down over the wounds, but without identifying the real malady*; this limited approach stops at the symptoms without going so far as to administer medicine for fear of disturbing the sick person. *On other occasions, mercy is likened to tolerance of evil*, which pretends not to see things and is unable to liberate the person from the evil in question. *Beyond mere compassion and tolerance there is biblical mercy which, as a work of God, is capable of renewing the person's heart, purifying it of all evil.* This mercy not only has compassion but cures; it not only tolerates but transforms. Mercy enables the sinner to return to life according to the covenant (cf. AL 64), that is to say, according to God's promise that is faithful and forever. Let us not forget that *the greatest misery, in which mercy shows that it is even greater, is estrangement from God*, which deprives a human being of the possibility of attaining his final end. The greatest misery is the loss of the great life that the Father promised us in Jesus. This correct understanding of mercy is fundamental if we want to avoid the fatal error that St. Paul describes: those who do not recognize that God's kindness is meant to lead them to repentance presume upon "the riches of his kindness and forbearance and patience" (cf. Rom 2:4).

Let us understand therefore the reason why, *although we are all sinners, these divorced persons find themselves in a peculiar situation and must make a special journey to be integrated into the Church.*

It is true that every Catholic, at the beginning of the Mass, declares, "I confess to Almighty God . . ." Similarly, before Communion, we repeat: "I am not worthy that you should come under my roof." St. Paul, moreover, enjoins us to make an examination of conscience in order to receive Communion worthily (cf. 1 Cor 11:28–29). In fact, as the Council of Trent teaches, someone who is aware of having committed a mortal sin must confess it before receiving the Eucharist.[9]

Nevertheless, some sins are obvious, because they have to do with visible relationships, one's concrete way of living in the community and of weaving one's own story. This is why Jesus decided to give clear instructions to the Apostles about how to deal with these errors, admonishing the sinners so that they might change their life (cf. Mt 18:15–17). *Amoris laetitia* adopts this perspective: the difficulty in participating fully in the Church and in being able to approach the Eucharist may lie in visible sins that affect the social body of the Church (cf. AL 185–186). *It is necessary, therefore, not only to "discern the Spirit," but also to "discern the body"* (cf. AL 185, which cites 1 Cor 11:29[10])—in other words, *to discern the concrete way in which we are living our relationships and, in particular, our fidelity to the indissoluble conjugal bond.*

This applies *in a special way to matrimony*, since in this case *we have a sacrament*, a visible and efficacious sign of grace. Marriage is not a private fact, much less an institution that involves only the husband, the wife, and the children. It is, instead, an essential element for the common life and for the edification of the Church.[11]

This explains the reason why these divorced persons must complete a journey before they can be fully integrated into ecclesial life and receive Holy Communion. In any case, these persons

---

[9] Cf. Council of Trent, *Decree on the Sacrament of the Eucharist*, Session 13, chapter 7, *DH* 1647.

[10] The conclusion is clear, as AL 186 points out: "The Eucharist demands that we be members of the one body of the Church. Those who approach the Body and Blood of Christ may not wound that same Body . . ."

[11] Cf. *Catechism of the Catholic Church* 1617.

must not feel offended when the Church tells them that they cannot approach the Eucharist because, as Pope Francis already reminded us in *Evangelii gaudium* 47, "The Eucharist is not a prize for the perfect" (cf. AL 300; 305). In other words, the Church does not declare that those who receive Holy Communion are perfect, nor should they consider themselves better than the others.

4. A SACRAMENTAL ITINERARY

The journey that *Amoris laetitia* seeks to set out on is based on accompaniment. In the preceding chapter we saw the various stages that make it possible to travel it; these are inspired by the catechumenate of the first centuries of the Church. As we had occasion to note, *the times of this journey cannot be planned in advance*, since we are talking about the work of renewing the heart, which is in God's hands: in that case, one does not measure the *chronos* of the clock but rather waits on the *kairos* of the Lord's merciful action upon our freedom. It will be a journey of integration into the sacraments, so as to make it possible to be fully integrated into the Church. It is necessary to recall that *the problem of these persons is not only interior but affects their concrete, visible relationships, inasmuch as they have adopted a way of loving that is opposed to conjugal love.* The difficulty, therefore, is sacramental, since the sacraments affect our body, our concrete situation in the flesh. Only when we are willing to conform our relationships to the Word of Christ can we receive the grace that allows us to be converted and to follow him. Otherwise, we run the risk of resembling those who hear the Word of God but do not put it into practice (cf. Mt 7:26): they do not yet follow the Master since they have not built their house on the rock of his grace—in other words, they have not sufficiently *integrated* Christian discipleship in its sacramental dimension.

These are precisely the objective situations that must be transformed patiently, since only in that way will God be able to renew the life of a human being, body and soul. It is true that God continues to act even when the person is living in a situation opposed to the Gospel, just as the seed continues to have potentiality even when the soil surrounding it is arid and poor. Nevertheless, it is likewise true that when the soil is not right, the seed can neither sprout nor put out roots so as to then produce fruit. The action of grace follows the logic of the Incarnation: it is not content with transforming us interiorly, but it wants to shape our concrete way of relating to one another in the body and of living in society. It is like the farmer who, turning over and fertilizing the soil, reaches the heart of the seed so that it can sprout.

This journey leads to harmony between the person's life, his or her concrete way of forming relationships, and the life of Christ. As the Council of Trent teaches, following the traditional practice of the Church, the journey must pass first of all through the Sacrament of Penance [Reconciliation] and, only then, lead to the Eucharist.[12] Recall that classical theology distinguished between the sacraments of the dead (Baptism and Reconciliation, which give eternal life to those who are in mortal sin, provided that they have the intention of changing their ways) and the sacraments of the living (such as the Eucharist, which forgives venial sins but can be received fruitfully only after having confessed serious sins). The necessity of sacramental confession is due, once again, to the fact that the Eucharist is not just a private matter, for which it would be enough to repent and to ask forgiveness of God in solitude. *The ecclesial dimension is necessary, because in the Eucharist the Church professes before the whole world the way of life that Jesus taught us.* In other words, in the Eucharist a common good of the Church and her public confession of faith are at stake.

Some wonder whether it is not unjust to exclude these persons for such a long time from the normal economy of grace, that is, from the sacraments. Well, then, let us remember that the journey on which these baptized persons set out is a journey of

[12] Cf. Council of Trent, *Decree on the Sacrament of the Eucharist*, Session 13, chapter 7, *DH* 1646–1647: "Whoever desires to communicate must be reminded of the precept 'Let a man examine himself' [*1 Cor 11:28*]. The practice of the Church declares that examination necessary, so that no one who is aware of personal mortal sin, however contrite he may feel, should approach the Holy Eucharist without first having made a sacramental confession." An exception is foreseen in the case in which no confessor is available, provided that the person resolves to make a sacramental confession as soon as possible.

reconciliation and, therefore, a sacramental journey. Penance, in fact, is a sacrament that extends through time, as we are reminded by the example of the prodigal son in his journey to the father's house. The matter of this sacrament consists of the acts of the penitent, which already include the first movement toward conversion. Consequently, those who are moving toward reconciliation and are accompanied by the Church along this journey are already receiving in a certain way the "help of the sacrament" (cf. AL 305, note 351), although they cannot yet be absolved of their sins.

We must recall that, precisely by virtue of the fact that this is a sacramental journey, God is the one who initiates and continues it. The pastor should be perfectly aware of the fact that he is not the protagonist of the journey: his role consists of facilitating the divine work. Since it is a sacramental way, we travel it with all of our frailty, but also and most importantly with all the hope that we have placed in God's action. Arriving at the finish line may seem impossible when we are taking the first steps, just as it seems impossible to those who are far from the fireplace to believe in the warmth of the fire. Nevertheless, *little by little, while they advance, while they participate in the prayer and revive their knowledge of Christ, they begin to be capable of receiving Jesus' strength* and, insofar as they are converted to God, can manage to live as he lived.

5. THE ITINERARY OF REPENTANCE

We have seen that, on this return path, it is not necessary to worry too much about time. The journey may be long or short, because God himself is the one who traces it out and brings it to completion. The important thing is not the time that it takes, but rather, as the Pope says, the "small steps" that are taken in order to draw closer to the goal, which always is life according to the promise made on the wedding day (cf. AL 271; 300; 305). This ultimate goal is undeniable: the Church is called to support "the way of grace and of growth" and "paths of sanctification which give glory to God" (AL 305).

Along this journey, the confessor plays an important role with his counsels and encouragement, while still monitoring the progress made and removing obstacles. Since these are long processes, in which many times the person is coming from a life that is estranged from the faith, it will be necessary to offer patient accompaniment so that the persons can prepare themselves for confession. Consequently, *if the priest who receives the penitent is an occasional confessor, for instance at a shrine or a basilica, the best thing for him to do is to refer him or her to a pastor qualified to deal with family matters who can give regular counsel.*

It is important to help persons to tell the story of their life, recalling the wrong that they have done, so as to ask forgiveness from God. Only by accepting and acknowledging our own story can we be freed from the guilt that torments us and does not allow us to look to the future. This is why *Confession consists not of telling the story from one's own perspective, but of setting it alongside the story of Jesus, "who loved me and gave himself for me"* (Gal 2:20). The priest, in Confession, represents Christ and helps the penitent to look at his or her story in terms of Christ's forgiveness. This is the reason why, at the moment of absolution, he recalls Jesus' work for us: "God, the Father of mercies, through the death and resurrection of his Son has reconciled the world to himself and sent the Holy Spirit among us for the forgiveness of sins; through the ministry of the Church may God give you pardon and peace, and I absolve you from your sins . . ."

Even in regard to divorced persons who are living in a new union, confession is meant to lead them to the point where they can accept as the measure of their own story the story of Jesus, which is the story of a "Yes forever" and of forgiveness "in spite of everything." In the case of these divorced persons, it is a matter of recognizing that the indissoluble bond that had united them in matrimony is the only firm foundation to which they can return in order to build their life, since this bond testifies to the truth of the love "forever" and "in spite of everything" that Jesus promised us. If we live in a way that contradicts this bond, our story will always be a fragmented story, because we will have set ourselves against this promise that conferred unity on all our steps, based on God's action.

Consequently, *in order to be able to give absolution, the confessor must make sure that the person is willing to leave this situation, that is, to abandon the foundations set in the shifting sands so as to begin building on the rock*, while allowing his or her story to be illuminated by the way in which Christ himself lived. As we will see in the final part of this book, it is not a matter of discerning the subjective guilt of the penitent, but rather of understanding whether he or she is willing to accept the objective (i.e., bodily, sacramental) form of Jesus' life. In the case of divorced persons who have remarried civilly, this means abandoning their way of living in relationship and of telling their own story—a way that contradicts the relations and the story of Christ.

Consequently, absolution will be given only when the person is willing to transform his or her visible and bodily relations according to the truth of the bond. Granting absolution ahead of time would mean harming the penitent: it is as though a physician allowed a patient who had broken a leg to walk before the bone had finally mended. This attitude would be harmful also to the common good of the Church, because it would be tantamount to denying that it is possible in practice to live with the indissolubility of marriage. In doing so, in fact, one would be following a logic of mere tolerance that does not allow the persons to be healed of their malady and, furthermore, one would fall into a clear application of gradualness of the law, under the pretense of making this situation (which is contrary to Jesus' words) "good enough."

This explains why the document speaks so much about "mitigating factors" (AL 301–303). Knowing that there are mitigating circumstances that may eliminate part of the persons' responsibility is important to avoid judging and/or feeling superior to them. Recall that nowadays, in an age when the culture of the family is lacking, society abandons persons right at the moment when they must build their life and their love, particularly when difficult situations arise. This is why many of them are not so much guilty parties as victims of an emotional society that does not enable them to build lasting relationships. Therefore, considering the mitigating factors helps us not to form harsh judgments and not to feel superior to these brothers and sisters who have been shipwrecked in the postmodern deluge.

Among the factors that mitigate the seriousness of irregular situations, we can mention ignorance, which may lead to an erroneous conscience. It is necessary to recall that absolution cannot be given based on the fact that the penitent's conscience is erroneous and, consequently, without guilt. That would mean seriously confusing the aspect of subjective guilt and the aspect of the sacramental forum. Of course, those who follow their invincibly erroneous conscience commit no sin at that moment, but this does not mean that their action is good, or that they do no evil. The persons' conscience is erroneous because they were influenced by social customs or by their internal disorders; it is therefore vitally important to do everything possible to help them to emerge from that darkness. For precisely this reason, having an invincibly erroneous conscience does not justify receiving absolution. The sacramental forum cannot be identified with the erroneous conscience, because if that were the case, the Church would lose every possibility of helping persons to emerge from the darkness that envelops them. Furthermore, if the Church were to identify the "I absolve you" with the erroneous conscience, then the Church herself would end up sinking into that darkness, about which Jesus says: "If then the light in you is darkness, how great is the darkness!" (Mt 6:23).

6. ON THE WAY TO THE EUCHARIST

Full participation in the Church, that is, the purpose of the journey of integration, coincides with full participation in the Eucharist, since this is the sacrament of the Church's unity. Accompaniment aims, therefore, at this gradual approach to the Eucharistic table, which the father prepares for the prodigal son after having placed the ring on his finger and clothed him with the wedding garment. Pope Francis rightly declares that "the Eucharist demands that we be members of the one body of the Church" (AL 186). As long as the integration is not full, because a person continues to live in a way opposed to their baptismal and marital promises, it will not be possible to allow that person to approach the Eucharist.

Let us recall, in this connection, the approach of St. Augustine who asked those who approached the sacraments not only to profess how Christ had lived, died, and risen, but also to confess how the members of the Body of Christ wish to live. This is why, when the priest says "The Body of Christ" and we respond "Amen," this means, according to St. Augustine: "Amen," so be it, I want my way of life, my way of relating to God and to other human beings to have the same foundations that Jesus laid.[13]

Certainly we do not mean imitating Jesus perfectly in my life (something that can happen only after traveling a long way—and never perfectly on this earth) but rather accepting Jesus' own foundations, his own basic coordinates, accomplishing the type of initial conversion that allows us to follow him.

Those who live contrary to the Sacrament of Matrimony, relating to someone who is not their spouse as if that were the case, are not yet ready to embrace this way of life; they are not ready to say "Amen." We can be certain that, in order to eat the Body of Christ, it is necessary to be willing to eat the words of Christ. Those who are not yet ready to assimilate his words will not be able to assimilate his Body either. St. Thomas maintained that, if the Church administered the sacrament to someone who was not ready to receive it, it would be like doing violence to him or her: it would force that person to adopt a way of life that he or she does not yet accept with docility.[14]

The relation between the Eucharist and Matrimony is the basis for this discipline of the Church, as recalled by St. Pope John Paul II in *Familiaris consortio* 84, by Benedict XVI in *Sacramentum Caritatis* 29, and by the document issued by the Congregation for the Doctrine of the Faith in 1994.[15] This relation is explained also by Pope Francis:

---

[13] Augustine, *Sermo*, PL 38, 272, 1.

[14] Cf. Thomas Aquinas, *Summa theologiae*, III, q. 68, art. 4, ad 3.

[15] Congregation for the Doctrine of the Faith, *Letter to the Bishops of the Catholic Church Concerning the Reception of Holy Communion by the Divorced and Remarried Members of the Faithful* (September 14, 1994).

> Jesus knocks on the door of families, to share with them the Eucharistic supper (cf. Rev 3:20). There, spouses can always seal anew the paschal covenant which united them and which ought to reflect the covenant which God sealed with mankind on the cross. The Eucharist is the sacrament of the new covenant, where Christ's redemptive work is carried out (cf. Lk 22:20). The close bond between married life and the Eucharist thus becomes all the more clear (AL 318; cf. also AL 38, 223).

Does all this mean that the journey of our brothers and sisters toward full integration into the Church must be made apart from the Eucharist? Absolutely not. The Eucharist is the very structure of the Church, and therefore if they participate in some way in the Body of Christ, they participate also in that same way in the Eucharist, and they can be active during the liturgy. In reality, the Eucharist draws them from the beginning of their journey and works in them, opening them to God's action so that he can renew their desires and lead them back to fullness. Recall that God grants us also what we sometimes do not even dare to ask for, and comes to the aid of our frailty, because we do not know how to ask as we ought.

The old catechumenate contained a symbol that represented this journey toward the Eucharist: the salt that was given to the catechumens. The catechumens could not go to communion, sometimes for long years, because they had to change their ways that were contrary to the Gospel, and therefore they needed time to complete this step. The salt, as St. Augustine explains, symbolized the desire for bread, the anticipated taste of the future Eucharistic banquet that attracted him and impelled him along his journey.[16]

In this connection it would be helpful to propose the practice of spiritual communion, as was suggested during the Synod (cf. *Relatio Synodi* 2014, n. 53). Those who cannot yet approach

---

[16] Cf. Bernard Botte, "Sacramentum catechumenorum," *Questions liturgiques et paroissiales* 43 (1962): 322–330.

the Eucharist can still nourish their desire to receive Christ and, in that way, become open to the action of grace. Although the person does not notice it, the desire to receive Jesus is connected with the desire to live according to his words and, consequently, according to the Sacrament of Matrimony that was received. Thus, the growth of a true Eucharistic desire will clear the way so that the desire to live in the truth of Matrimony will grow too. The yearning from Communion must go hand in hand with the desire for the Lord to renew one's heart, so that one can live according to the Sacrament of Matrimony. Indeed, remember that the Sacrament of the Eucharist does not mean only the interior union of the believer with his God. This is, first and foremost, a sacrament that concerns the flesh and tends to influence all our relationships. Consequently it is a sacrament that visibly represents Jesus' love for his Church. It is necessary to note, furthermore, that this method of integration follows the law of gradualness perfectly, since it aims at the gradual purification of the person's desire.

7. CLARIFICATIONS OF SOME FOOTNOTES OF THE DOCUMENT THAT HAVE BEEN MISINTERPRETED

Some have claimed to see in footnotes 336 and 351 a change in the Eucharistic discipline for divorced and "remarried" persons. Is that really the case?

Footnote 336 refers to the passage: "the consequences or effects of a rule need not necessarily always be the same" (AL 300). The footnote explains: "This is also the case with regard to sacramental discipline, since discernment can recognize that in a particular situation no grave fault exists."

Should this idea be applied also to the norm stated by *Familiaris consortio* 84 concerning divorced persons who have remarried civilly? In order to answer this question, it is necessary to observe first of all that, in this situation, the document simply says that the norms in sacramental discipline do *not necessarily* involve the same consequences for everyone. Consequently, it does not rule out (and this is why it uses the adverb *necessarily*) the possibility that some norms may have the same effects for everyone, and this is precisely what happens with the norm established by *Familiaris consortio* 84 and confirmed by *Sacramentum Caritatis* 29, which does not depend on the subjective culpability of the person. The idea was then clarified by no less than the Pontifical Council for the Interpretation of Legislative Texts, which is cited as a source by *Amoris laetitia* (AL 302, note 345). Let us take another example of a sacramental norm that is applied in every case: the fact that one must receive Baptism before being admitted to the Eucharist; this is a norm that is valid in all cases, since it does not depend on the subjective culpability of the person. What norms, then, are referred to in this footnote 336? The answer to this question is contained in the preceding context: the document just spoke (AL 299) about norms regarding sacramental discipline, such as the choice of godfathers or godmothers, the job of lector and acolyte; in other words, norms that also have to do with integration into the Church.

As far as footnote 351 is concerned, it states that in some cases the Church could offer the help of the sacraments to someone who is living in an objectively sinful situation, if he or she were not subjectively guilty or not fully responsible. The document refers generally to objective conditions of sin, without specifying that these are manifest, or that the person stubbornly remains in them. These two requirements, specifically mentioned in CIC 915, make it impossible to absolve and to admit to the Eucharist divorced persons in a new union, because they are putting at risk the common good of the Church and her public, visible profession of the word of Jesus.

Moreover: the case of the divorced and "remarried" is quite specific, since in it the couple is living in a way that contradicts the reality of the Sacrament of Matrimony and the bond that it creates. For reasons of internal sacramental logic it is impossible that someone who is living in contradiction to one sacrament (Matrimony) should actually want to receive another sacrament (the Eucharist). The very force of the Eucharistic desire ought to lead the person to abandon his or her way of life that is contrary to Matrimony.

From all this it is necessary to conclude that footnote 351 is very general. It would be valid, therefore, in objectively sinful situations that are not manifest, that do not involve the person's stubborn insistence on remaining in it, and do not directly contradict a sacrament. The manual for confessors by the Pontifical Council for the Family made specific reference to some of these cases.[17] This footnote cannot be applied to the case of divorced persons who have remarried civilly, for whom there is a very clear Magisterial teaching that serves as a sure guide to clarify any doubt.

8. WHAT, THEN, ARE THE NEW WAYS OPENED UP BY THE APOSTOLIC EXHORTATION?

Anyone who thinks that the *new ways* for the family offered by the Synods and proposed by the Pope boil down to establishing *new norms* either has an exaggerated idea of what a *norm* is, or else a too limited idea of what a *way of salvation* is. The new ways mentioned by Pope Francis refer to changes in the hearts of persons and ask the Church for a "pastoral conversion,"[18] that is to say, they ask the Church to make the pastoral care of the family a central concern and activity in every diocese and every parish. These ways can be opened neither by a decree nor by a document, but by common effort aimed at approaching these brothers and sisters and accompanying them along their journey toward Christ.

In this context *Amoris laetitia* encourages us to undertake two journeys: a) it asks us to start a process of full reintegration into the Church for persons who have become estranged from it (cf. AL 291), a process that must be guided by the diocesan bishop, as the Pope asks, repeating the words of the Synod (AL 300); b) it encourages confessors, when they are ascertaining whether the person truly wants to start to live according to the Gospel, to

[17] Cf. Pontifical Council for the Family, *Vademecum for Confessors Concerning Some Aspects of the Morality of Conjugal Life* (February 12, 1997).

[18] Cf. Francis, *Evangelii gaudium*, n.25.

keep in mind the mitigating factors, so as to evaluate their resolution benevolently, according to the logic of small steps of growth, as called for by the law of gradualness (AL 301–306).

9. HOW CAN WE ENCOURAGE THESE DIVORCED PERSONS ON THEIR JOURNEY TOWARD FULLER PARTICIPATION?

While they continue along this journey, participating in the life of the community in prayer and in works of mercy, and giving witness to the Gospel in their work and in educating their children, these brethren of ours receive God's help. It is true that the Eucharist is a medicine against sin, but it is likewise true, as the wise Franciscan St. Bonaventure declared, "sometimes postponing the remedy is a medical act"[19] because there are medicines which, if taken prematurely, do more harm than good.

Indeed, the very impossibility of receiving Holy Communion is a medicine for divorced and remarried persons on their journey toward integration. This is true, first of all, because it reminds them that there is a problem in the way that they are establishing and living out their visible relationships; it reminds them likewise that this situation is an obstacle to their growth in charity toward God and neighbor. And this gives rise to uneasiness in them: they cannot stop where they are, because that would mean cutting themselves off from the goal; therefore they have ahead of them a journey to make. Since we are talking about a sacramental journey, this journey refers to the very structure of their personal relations in the body, which are in contradiction to the words of Jesus and to the way in which he himself embodied love.

Furthermore, these divorced and remarried persons must think of the good that they do for others when they remain faithful to this discipline. *Amoris laetitia* suggests that they ask themselves what sort of example their new union sets "for young people who are preparing for marriage" (AL 300). Clearly, if they

[19] Cf. Bonaventure, *In Quartum Librum Sententiarum*, d. 18, pars 2, articulus unicus, q. 1, resp. 3 (in *Opera omnia* IV [Florence, Quaracchi, 1889], 485).

went to Communion, they would give a bad example: the young people would think their love is not forever, that there are cases in which the Church ceased to fight to defend their bond. It is necessary to think also of the families who are going through difficult times and may even be thinking of breaking up: if they saw that others, although living in contradiction to their marriage, were welcomed by the Church, they too would feel authorized to take the same route. In short, divorced persons in a new union who agree not to receive the Eucharist provide a service to the common good of all families.

This is true also for the education of their children in the faith. The parents' decision not to go to Communion has great educational value for their children and shows the courage of the parents in giving a real testimony of their faith. Thus, the children will learn that their parents, although they were weak in making their choices, are capable of witnessing to the truth of a life in which God is important. This is an educational "word" pronounced in an era in which young people need, above all, not suffocating emotions that imprison them, but rather a simple, solid witness to the possibility of building a life based on true love. The Church, with her Eucharistic discipline, supports these parents in their task of raising children in the faith, as the Pope asks us (cf. AL 246).

Recall, finally, that the place par excellence in which the Church professes her faith is the Eucharist. It is here that we profess the Creed every Sunday, and in the Eucharistic discipline we give witness to the special way of life that Jesus taught us. Consequently, with regard to the Eucharistic discipline, divorced and "remarried" persons keep their faith alive and join in with the whole Church in professing it. This faith, in fact, is not just an abstract doctrine, as the Holy Father reminds us (AL 36), and these persons, by upholding the Eucharistic discipline, profess the Church's living faith in the efficacious words of Jesus. If the Church behaved differently, she would be committing a "falsehood in the sacramental signs," as St. Thomas Aquinas declares.[20]

---

[20] Cf. Thomas Aquinas, *Summa theologiae*, III, q. 68, art. 4.

In other words, yielding on this point would not mean opening a gate in the wall so as to admit more people, but rather would mean making a hole in the keel of a ship, of the Noah's Ark that is the Church, which therefore would end up sinking irremediably.

The priest who claims to have acted out of mercy by allowing a divorced and "remarried" person to approach the Eucharist, without fulfilling the conditions spelled out by FC 84, perhaps does not think that other couples in his parish, who may be experiencing temptations to infidelity or to leave their spouse, upon learning of this way of proceeding, might think that their actions are not that serious and might yield to the temptation to abandon their family? Because of a false idea of mercy, this priest endangers the fidelity of families, the common good of the Church, and the Church's witness as the light of the world (cf. Mt 5:14).

The Eucharistic discipline of the Church is a great service of mercy with regard to these brothers and sisters of ours, whom the Church does not consider second-class Christians or as incapable of living the fullness of Jesus' words. Following the Synod, Pope Francis declares, "The way of the Church is not to condemn anyone forever" (AL 296). In other words, the Church always keeps hope alive: it is possible to return to life according to the Gospel, that is, to the full life that Jesus promised. We must not give in to the temptation to think that this is not feasible: "Can such generosity . . . be possible? Yes, because it is demanded by the Gospel" (AL 102).

10. INTEGRATING: BUILDING ONE'S HOUSE UPON THE ROCK

Along their journey leading to full participation in the life of the Church, persons who have divorced and remarried civilly are accompanied not only by the priest: the whole Christian community is called to support them (cf. AL 246), offering them first of all the witness of family life founded on Christ. This is what it means to integrate ecclesially. This witness will be humble, since it acknowledges human weakness, and at the same time it will be full of hope, because it experiences God's power. Once again it is necessary to recall that families are the acting subjects of pastoral activity and that the space that they create is the fertile ground of the common household, that is, the space that enables all whose love has lost its way (cf. AL 291) to turn back and build on solid foundations. In secularized society, the family setting is now missing, and families live without the help of a society that supports them (AL 32). This is a profound misfortune for the family, because many times it is forced to encapsulate itself in a bubble of relationships, as though it were an island, whereas its vocation is to be open: the husband and the wife are open to life and to the generation of a common good (cf. AL, chapter six). Without a society that supports it, the family cannot continue to exist. In this context we find a great challenge for the Church: to build a culture of the family, a fabric of good practices, traditions, spaces for fellowship that help to support the desire for a family (AL 1) and for true love (AL 294) that dwells in the heart of every person. If she wants to be a community that integrates, the Church must build a common house upon solid foundations in the midst of the individualistic desert of contemporary society.

To conclude this chapter, we wish to cite a Gospel image: the house built on the rock that withstands the hurricane. *Amoris laetitia* applies this contrast to two types of families that Francis intends to address: two types of families created by the freedom of their members (cf. AL 8). Families built on the rock are founded on Christ; those built on sand run the risk of seeing their house collapse because they have abandoned the plans of the wise architect.

It is interesting to learn that there are two versions of this parable: one is related by St. Matthew and the other by St. Luke. According to St. Matthew (Mt 7:24–29) there are two different terrains: the rock and the sand. Building on the rock means taking Jesus' words as the foundation; listening to his words without putting them into practice is tantamount to building on sand. The passage is found at the end of the Sermon on the Mount, in which Jesus says, among other things, that "Everyone who divorces his wife, except on the ground of unchastity [i.e. an illegitimate union], makes her an adulteress; and whoever marries a divorced woman commits adultery" (Mt 5:32). The greatest mercy one can offer to someone who has built on sand, ignoring these words of Jesus, is to help him to take the stones out of the sand and to place them on solid rock.

In contrast, St. Luke (Lk 6:47–49) distinguishes not by the terrain, but rather by the depth of the construction. Here the problem is different: the foundation of the building is not deep enough to reach the rock. With this type of person it is not necessary to require uprooting; it is enough to lay a deeper foundation.

The two parables distinguish two types of family situations, and they too offer a path toward the Church. Those who are living in a manifest, stable situation that is contrary to Jesus' words (divorced and "remarried" persons, civil marriage, cohabitation . . .) must be warned that they are building on sand. In that case, the only way out is to abandon that terrain, that is to say, the situation in which they find themselves. In order to do that it is necessary to make the journey that we have described. Patiently and tactfully, it is necessary to communicate to these persons that the desire for true love that they have in their hearts cannot bloom on that terrain, that is, by forming relationships in that way. The persons must therefore be uprooted from that place so as to adopt the plan designed by the divine architect, since this is the only plan to follow in order to build a solid edifice that is capable of withstanding the storms of the present time.

Once the persons have settled down on the rock, it is necessary to carry out another task, the one pointed out to us by St. Luke: descending ever deeper into the rock, which is Christ, so as to have the best possible foundation. Subsequently the house can be expanded, and therefore the family will be able to show its special fruitfulness and be capable of welcoming other families, of supporting them in times of difficulty, and of creating the atmosphere and the culture of the family. This is the ultimate objective of the whole process of integration: not only to make sure that the person can become an integral part of the Church, but also that he or she can help generate the Church, creating spaces where others can come to live, like the tree in the Gospel parable in whose branches the birds of the air can come and make their nests (Mt 13:31–32).

CHAPTER THREE

Discerning: A Path in the Light of Truth

WHEN Pope Francis speaks about discernment, he does so while citing paragraph 84 of the Post-Synodal Apostolic Exhortation *Familiaris consortio* by St. Pope John Paul II: "Pastors must know that, for the sake of truth, they are obliged to exercise careful discernment of situations."[1] This passage, which is found both in *Familiaris consortio* and in *Amoris laetitia*, raises an obvious question: if situations require discernment, which is to say, if the situations are different, then shouldn't the respective solutions be different too? Thus, when John Paul II writes that there is "a difference between those who have sincerely tried to save their first marriage and have been unjustly abandoned, and those who through their own grave fault have destroyed a canonically valid marriage,"[2] should we not immediately expect that he will continue by proposing different solutions for each case? Nevertheless, this is not what he actually does. After calling for careful discernment, he continues to speak in very general terms about "divorced persons who have remarried,"[3] emphasizing that they cannot be admitted to the Eucharist.

---

1 John Paul II, *Familiaris consortio*, n. 84; AL 79.

2 John Paul II, *Familiaris consortio*, n. 84.

3 Ibid.

For John Paul II, the reasons for this practice result from the fact that "their state and condition of life objectively contradict that union of love between Christ and the Church which is signified and effected by the Eucharist"—in a way that is altogether independent of the questions that he had just raised a few lines earlier, namely whether they had been unjustly abandoned or had more or less voluntarily destroyed their marriage by their own fault. Moreover, when the Polish Pope then goes on to explain the conditions based on which access to the sacraments may be allowed even to those who "for serious reasons such as for example the children's upbringing . . . cannot satisfy the obligation to separate," namely by abstaining "from the acts proper to married couples,"[4] he once again talks about *all* divorced persons in a new union, regardless of any previous discernment.

If there is only one solution, why would there ever be a need for discernment? Did John Paul II simply contradict himself in a rather obvious manner? One very probable answer is as follows: even though there is only one solution or *goal*, discernment will still be necessary in order to find the *way* to get there, and in this case the circumstances through which persons have come to find themselves in a specific situation will be of great importance. Indeed, one of our main theses in this chapter is that discernment has to do with the path and not the goal. This is clearly the case in *Familiaris consortio* 84. Given that Pope Francis bases his argument explicitly on this paragraph, it will be quite plausible to understand the indications about discernment provided by *Amoris laetitia* in the same light, even though *Amoris laetitia* in fact goes beyond *Familiaris consortio* precisely by being more explicit about the concrete path of discernment, offering a new and original contribution.

We will proceed basically in two stages. First, on a negative note, we will reflect on what discernment does not mean. Next we will examine in a positive way the actual meaning of the term. Throughout the discussion we will be guided by the text of *Amoris laetitia* itself, by the documents that are cited in it and by its

---

[4] Ibid.

genesis, interpreting the difficult passages in the context of the whole document, in the context of its Magisterial sources, and in the context of the Synods. Consequently, we will argue that discernment does *not* mean

- judging a person's state of grace, or
- evaluating a person's concrete possibilities so as to adapt the moral law to them.

Then we will continue by suggesting that discernment *does mean*

- with regard to its *goal*: identifying ways of living according to the truth of one's marriage bond;
- with regard to its *modality*: thinking and feeling in harmony with the Church; and
- with regard to its *object*: the discernment of desire, of the marriage bond, and of concrete steps.

1. DISCERNMENT DOES NOT MEAN JUDGING A PERSON'S STATE OF GRACE

In *Amoris laetitia* Francis emphasizes that persons encounter many difficulties and that there are mitigating factors on account of which "it can no longer simply be said that all those in any 'irregular' situation are living in a state of mortal sin and are deprived of sanctifying grace" (AL 301). Some saw in this statement an argument in favor of possibly admitting to the sacraments at least some of the divorced living in a new union. They claimed that we have gained a new awareness, which should lead to a new praxis. In what follows we would like to highlight the fact that in reality this teaching is not new and that the question of admission to Holy Communion has never involved a judgment about a person's state of grace. Therefore, the above-cited passage cannot serve to support a change of the current praxis. Instead, in the passage under discussion, Francis refers to a firm teaching of the Tradition and Magisterium of the Church. In reality, *it has never been possible to say that* what Francis states *can no longer be said.* In *Ecclesia de Eucharistia,* for example, John Paul II writes: "The judgment of one's state of grace obviously belongs only to the person involved, since it is a question of examining one's conscience."[5]

Therefore when Francis emphasizes that pastoral discernment must be dynamic (cf. AL 303), the text could perhaps have been clearer. It is not entirely apparent what needs to be discerned. Is the Pope really asking pastors of souls to discern (and "discern" is really just a synonym for "judge") a person's state of grace? That really would be a novelty, and rather ironic to boot. It would mean that the very Pope who memorably asked, "Who am I to judge?" was inviting the priests of the Church to issue a sort of judgment on their penitents that St. Thomas Aquinas described as "rash." Aside from the fact that Thomas is the Common Doctor of the Church, a reference to him is appropriate also because Pope Francis stresses that "everything [written in *Amoris laetitia*] is Thomist, from beginning to end."[6] Now, in Thomas' view there are numerous conditions for rash judgment, and one of them is that "a person presumes to judge about hidden matters, of which God alone has the power to judge."[7] He explains that while God "has entrusted us with judging externals, . . . he has reserved internals to himself. . . . For no one ought to judge that another is an evil man, for doubts must be interpreted in the more favorable light."[8] St. Thomas is speaking therefore about the impossibility of judging another person's state of grace.

The Council of Trent speaks about the impossibility of judging with certainty even *one's own* state of grace when it declares: "No one can know with the certainty of faith, which cannot be subject to error, that he has obtained the grace of God."[9] Obvi-

---

[5] Pope John Paul II, Encyclical Letter On the Eucharist in Its Relationship to the Church *Ecclesia de Eucharistia* (April 17, 2003), n. 37.

[6] Pope Francis, *Address at the Opening of the Pastoral Congress of the Diocese of Rome* (June 16, 2016).

[7] Thomas Aquinas, *Commentary on the Letter of Paul to the Romans,* Latin-English Edition, trans. R. F. Larcher (Lander, WY: The Aquinas Institute for the Study of Sacred Doctrine, 2012), chapter 2, lesson 1, 174.

[8] Thomas Aquinas, *Super Evangelium S. Matthaei lectura,* chapter 7, lesson 1.

[9] Council of Trent, *Decree on Justification,* chapter 9, *DH* 1534.

ously this does not mean that we do not have to examine our consciences before receiving the Eucharist. It is important not to go to Communion while aware of a mortal sin that has not been confessed. And yet this is not the same as being certain that one is in the state of grace. One can hope to be, but one cannot have the certitude of faith. If this is the case with judging *one's own* soul, what can be said about discerning *someone else's* state of soul? Ultimately God is the one who judges the heart. The Church, on the other hand, has always limited herself to judging external conduct or objective states of life.

The preceding argument leads to two considerations. In the first place, since it would be rash judgment for a person to pass a negative judgment on someone else's state of grace, the Church in fact refrains from this type of judgment. Indeed, *her practice of not admitting divorced and civilly remarried persons to the Eucharist*—unless by resolving to live in abstinence they show an objective sign of repentance for having entered what is in fact an extramarital union—*is not the same as the judgment that they are living in a state of mortal sin.* It is a judgment on their state of life as one that objectively contradicts the mystery of the faithful union between Christ and his Church that is celebrated in the Eucharist. This is not a judgment on their souls, the condition of which is known only by God.

In the second place, it is necessary to ask oneself the following questions: If a negative judgment on a person's state of grace is rash, why shouldn't a positive judgment in this regard be rash too? How can anyone measure the weight of possible mitigating factors, social conditioning, and psychological limitations? To date no instrument has been found with which to measure empirically the presence or absence of grace, and it is not yet possible to determine on a case-by-case basis the extent of freedom with which a person commits a gravely immoral act. When the Church canonizes her saints, she follows a carefully regulated process. The most important thing is that the persons being examined must be deceased: *nemo ante mortem beatus* [no one is blessed before death]. During life they must have had the reputation of sanctity. Unless we are talking about martyrs, there is the requirement of certified miracles that can be attributed to the intercession of the candidates. Now, on what basis is a single pastor supposed to be able to declare blessed a person who is still alive, who lives in a public situation of objective sin, and who very probably is not a miracle worker? Or, in other words: how could a confessor be capable of discerning whether persons who are habitually and publicly unfaithful to their spouse are nevertheless living in God's grace? *By its very nature this type of judgment will always be rash and presumptuous.*

Except for the very special type of judgment pronounced after the process of beatification and canonization, the Church does not judge a person's state of grace. She can however judge the act itself. She can say that if persons perform certain *types* of acts—adultery, murder, pedophilia—with enough awareness and a sufficient degree of freedom, then this act will be such as to make them lose their friendship with God, because such an act radically contradicts the very essence of God who is the faithful Bridegroom of the Church, his Bride, the lover of life and the defender of the little ones. In other words, they commit a mortal sin. This is all that pastors of souls need to know and can know. Whether or not the adulterers, murderers, or pedophiles were mentally lucid when they committed that act, whether or not these persons had dominion over their actions when they acted, whether or not they truly separated themselves from God inasmuch as they were fully present to themselves in an act that is in itself hateful to God—all this God alone knows. Even though the confessor will certainly try to understand how free a given person was in fact—if only to be capable of giving useful advice and a suitable penance—in the end he will never be capable of measuring or determining precisely the degree of freedom with which the person acted and in what state of grace he or she has come to be ever since. Ultimately, the discernment of the heart is reserved to God alone. The priest in the confessional must discern the act; the state of the soul remains hidden to him.

It is obvious, therefore, that the Holy Father's words about discernment cannot be interpreted as an invitation to discern the state of grace of an individual faithful for the purpose of then admitting to Communion—in the case where the discernment was positive—persons who are in objectively sinful situations. The Pope would be asking the impossible (cf. the Council of Trent) and would be contradicting himself ("Who am I to judge?"). The pastor cannot declare his parishioners blessed before their death. Therefore, for him the question about whether they are in a state of grace cannot be answered. When it is a matter of possibly admitting to Communion divorced persons who are living in a new union, the question about the state of their souls is not even the decisive one. Certainly it is a necessary condition for all the faithful to examine their consciences (cf. 1 Cor 11) and to consider whether they are aware of having committed any mortal sins. Nevertheless, a positive (albeit always uncertain) judgment about the state of their soul by their conscience is not sufficient in itself. The question of admission to the Eucharistic banquet is not just a question of a person's state of soul, but also of his or her state of life, which in the case under discussion *publicly* contradicts the meaning of the Eucharist.

It is essential to understand what is meant by "admission" to the sacraments. "Admission" here has a *public* meaning. To say that persons are admitted to the sacraments does not mean that they automatically do well to approach them. Those who are admitted are those who should not be refused, while those who are not admitted are those who as a matter of principle ought to be refused, even in a public act. In addressing this problem, St. Thomas introduces the distinction between *secret* (or *occult*) and *notorious* (or *open*) sinners. Some persons are publicly known as gangsters, or have been denounced as criminals by some civil or ecclesiastical tribunal. For the Angelic Doctor, "Holy Communion ought not to be given to open sinners when they ask for it."[10] Nevertheless, and significantly, "But if they be not open sinners, but occult, the Holy Communion should not be denied them if they ask for it. For since every Christian, from the fact that he is baptized, is admitted to the Lord's table, he may not be robbed of his right, except from

[10] Thomas Aquinas, *Summa theologiae*, III, q. 80, art. 6.

some open cause."[11] We see that just as non-admission to the sacraments does not involve a judgment that a given person is in a state of mortal sin, so too the public admission to the Eucharist does not mean that a given person does well to receive the Eucharist.

It is still true that those who are aware of mortal sin and are not perfectly contrite must abstain from approaching the Eucharistic table.[12] To receive the Eucharist in such a condition would be to commit a sacrilege and therefore to add another serious sin to the preceding ones. If their sin is private, these persons should not be refused, that is to say, they should be admitted to Communion if they ask for it. The priest will not be obliged to refuse them the Eucharist. If for some reason he knows about a secret sin of a person, he "can privately warn the secret sinner, or warn all openly in public, from approaching the Lord's table, until they have repented of their sins and have been reconciled to the Church," but he should not refuse to give them Communion. Significantly, the reason that Aquinas mentions is not that the secret sinner deserves more "mercy" than the public one. Instead, the reason is that the act of refusing Communion to the private sinner would be tantamount to an act of defaming him which, for Thomas, is in itself a mortal sin. Even though the secret sinner, by receiving the Body of Christ unworthily, commits a mortal sin, the priest should not refuse him in that case, since "no one ought to commit mortal sin in order to keep another out of mortal sin."[13]

We have seen that the question of admission or non-admission to the Eucharist and to the other sacraments is a question that concerns a person's public state of life and not his or her private conscience. A private sinner must be admitted publicly. Not all those who are publicly admitted are thereby being declared saints. There could be some who are eating and drinking judgment upon themselves (cf. 1 Cor 11:29). Public sinners must

---

[11] Thomas Aquinas, *Summa theologiae*, III, q. 80, art. 6.

[12] It is a sign of perfect contrition when someone wants to confess his or her sins as soon as it is practically and morally possible. The mere fact of not going to confession when the sacrament is offered before Mass is usually in itself a sign that the person's contrition is not perfect.

[13] Thomas Aquinas, *Summa theologiae*, III, q. 80, art. 6, ad 2.

not be admitted, that is to say, as a matter of principle they ought to be refused. It does not follow from this that all who are not admitted are public sinners. For example, one could think of the catechumens, who need to wait patiently and receive Baptism first according to the order of the Church.

In this question about public admission to the sacraments, a personal examination of conscience will not be enough, nor will it be possible for the priest to scrutinize the person's heart. Ultimately it is a question that concerns someone's public state of life. For example, only God knows how much responsibility a person had for coming to be in a given notorious situation. The priest in the confessional can only know that a given living situation—for example membership in a terrorist organization—is objectively in contradiction to God's plan for that person, with his call to become a friend of God. If someone is capable of making choices, *if* the person has dominion over his or her acts and can take responsibility for his or her life, *then* this person will have to choose between being a friend of assassins or being a friend of God: how could anyone be the friend of a father and at the same time be the friend of those who kill his children? In this case there is an objective, public tension, even though the question about subjective responsibility remains unanswered. There is an objective, public tension also between wanting to celebrate the mystery of the Lord's fidelity to his Bride and being in a situation in which one is habitually and publicly unfaithful to one's spouse. This objective, public contradiction is entirely independent from the question of a person's individual, subjective responsibility.

So far we have discussed two points that we must hold on to: 1) it is impossible for someone to measure, discern, or judge the degree of freedom with which another human being is involved in an objectively sinful situation, and 2) with regard to the question of admission or non-admission to the sacraments—as public acts—the decisive thing is not the individual's state of grace or someone's subjective guilt, but rather his or her objective public condition.

Why is the question of the *public* nature of a state of life so important? We said that a *necessary* condition for someone to receive the Eucharist is that that person can say in his or her conscience: "I am not aware of any unconfessed mortal sin." Why can this not be the *sufficient* condition also? This of course is not a new question. The *Declaration Concerning the Admission to Holy Communion of Faithful Who are Divorced and Remarried* by the Pontifical Council for the Interpretation of Legislative Texts, which is a document cited also by *Amoris laetitia* (cf. AL 302, note 345), affirms that "the reception of the Body of Christ when one is publicly unworthy constitutes an objective harm to the ecclesial communion: it is a behavior that affects the rights of the Church and of all the faithful to live in accord with the exigencies of that communion."[14] The public nature of a given state of life creates a new situation that involves not only the individual conscience but the entire community of the Church.

Therefore, even before the Pontifical Council for Legislative Texts, the Congregation for the Doctrine of the Faith too had made a pronouncement with regard to the same problem, addressing in particular the question of whether "the divorced and remarried members of the faithful could approach Holy Communion in specific cases when they consider themselves authorised according to a judgement of conscience to do so."[15] The persons concerned may, for example, be convinced of the nullity of their earlier marriage and may even perceive their current extramarital union as a virtual gift from heaven, as a high-ranking prelate of the Church once said. The reason why private discernment in the internal forum is not sufficient is that "marriage . . . is essentially a public reality."[16] Indeed, "the consent that is the foundation of marriage is not simply a private decision since it creates a specifically ecclesial and social situation for the spouses, both individually and as a

[14] Pontifical Council for Legislative Texts, *Declaration Concerning the Admission to Holy Communion of Faithful Who are Divorced and Remarried* (June 24, 2000).

[15] Congregation for the Doctrine of the Faith, *Letter to the Bishops of the Catholic Church Concerning the Reception of Holy Communion by the Divorced and Remarried Members of the Faithful* (September 14, 1994), n. 3.

[16] Ibid., n. 7.

couple."[17] If marriage were a private affair, then a private judgment on its invalidity would be sufficient in order to attempt it again with someone else. Nevertheless, when spouses unite in matrimony, they do something that goes beyond themselves. They enter into a social and ecclesial institution. Therefore, "the judgment of conscience of one's own marital situation does not regard only the immediate relationship between man and God, as if one could prescind from the Church's mediation, that also includes canonical laws binding in conscience."[18] Being an ecclesial reality, marriage is mediated by the Church. It does not only concern each spouse's individual relationship with God, nor what the two feel and think about each other as a couple. To disregard the importance of the Church's mediation, which "also includes canonical laws binding in conscience," would mean "in fact to deny that marriage is a reality of the Church, that is to say, a sacrament."[19] Therefore the question about the nullity of a marriage requires discernment "by means of the external forum established by the Church."[20]

In the age of liberalism, Pope Francis warns against "an extreme individualism which weakens family bonds and ends up considering each member of the family as an isolated unit" (AL 33). From the individualistic perspective, society serves only to protect the citizens from one another. A community, then, is an aggregation of individuals. In this liberal approach, the Church is simply the aggregation of individual believers, each of whom has a personal relationship with Jesus. The Eucharist is therefore seen simply and exclusively as the moment of personal intimacy with the Lord. If my conscience, the innermost sanctuary where I stand alone before God, tells me that Jesus is all right with me, who can tell me otherwise? Who will prevent me from approaching him? From this perspective it will be utterly incomprehensible how the Church could attribute such great importance to the *public nature* of a particular state of life.

---

[17] Congregation for the Doctrine of the Faith, *Concerning the Reception of Holy Communion...*, n. 8.

[18] Ibid.

[19] Ibid.

[20] Ibid., n. 9.

Pope Francis, however, points out "the close bond between married life and the Eucharist" (AL 318). Just as matrimony is not just a private affair between me, my spouse, and Jesus, so too receiving the Eucharist is not simply a private matter. The Holy Father emphasizes that "to 'discern' the body of the Lord" means "to acknowledge it with faith and charity both in the sacramental signs and in the community" (AL 186). St. Paul's admonition not to take part in the Lord's Supper without "discerning the body" (cf. 1 Cor 11:29) cannot be understood as a reference to a question that regards the individual conscience alone. It is a discernment both of the Body of Christ present in the sacramental sign and also of the Body of Christ that is the Church. "The Eucharist demands that we be members of the one body of the Church" (AL 186). At a time when individualism threatens to influence many Catholics as well, the emphasis on the Church as the Body of Christ is extremely important: the Church is the "universal sacrament of salvation,"[21] "a sign and instrument . . . of communion with God and of unity among all men."[22] As a body, she is a living organism, the continuation of the Incarnation,[23] Christ's contemporaneity with the people of all ages.[24] In order to discern the Eucharist, we need to discern the Church, understanding ourselves as her members. As St. Ignatius of Loyola says, in order to discern we need to feel and to think with the Church, that is to say, we need to be steeped in her way of seeing things and to "put aside all judgment of our own, and keep the mind ever ready and prompt to obey in all things the true Spouse of Christ our Lord, our Holy Mother, the hierarchical Church."[25]

---

[21] Second Vatican Council, *Lumen gentium*, n. 48.

[22] Ibid., n. 1.

[23] Cf. Pope John Paul II, Encyclical Letter on Mother of the Redeemer *Redemptoris mater* (March 25, 1987), n. 5: "The reality of the Incarnation finds a sort of extension in the mystery of the Church—the Body of Christ."

[24] Cf. John Paul II, *Veritatis splendor*, n. 25, which reads in Latin: "Simultas temporum Christi cum homine cuiusvis aetatis fit in ipsius corpore, quod est Ecclesia." The official English translation unfortunately does not manage to convey this concept.

[25] This is the first of the Ignatian "rules for thinking with the Church," which are found at the end of *The Spiritual Exercises of St. Ignatius*, a new translation by Louis J. Puhl, S.J. (Westminster, MD: The Newman Press, 1959), 157.

All this goes to show that discernment is not just a matter between me and Jesus. Naturally Catholics believe that Jesus loves us personally and calls us by name individually. At the same time they believe that "one cannot have God as Father without having the Church as mother."[26] We are saved to the extent to which we are incorporated in Christ. We are saved to the extent to which we are members of his Body, the Church. Therefore, as Pope Francis emphasizes, discernment must be ecclesial. "We must not forget," he says, citing Benedict XVI, "that 'the "mysticism" of the sacrament has a social character'" (AL 186[27]).

2. DISCERNMENT DOES NOT MEAN EVALUATING THE PERSON'S CONCRETE POSSIBILITIES SO AS TO ADAPT THE MORAL LAW TO THEM

Discernment, therefore, does not mean discerning a person's subjective state of grace. Next we will argue that neither does it mean adapting the moral law to what persons perceive as their concrete possibilities. In fact many people, even within the Church, have misunderstood the moral law by considering it a burden on the conscience of the faithful. They then maintain that there are no definitive moral norms and believe that it is never possible to say with certainty what a person must or must not do. For them, discernment always depends on the situation. There is in truth a passage in *Amoris laetitia* that these people could use as an argument in their favor. In *Amoris laetitia* 305 we read: "Discernment must help to find possible ways of responding to God and growing in the midst of limits. By thinking that everything is black and white, we sometimes close off the way of grace and of growth, and discourage paths of sanctification which give glory to God." The Pope then continues in the same paragraph by citing a passage from his Apostolic Letter *Evangelii gaudium*: "Let us remember that 'a small step, in the midst of great human limitations, can

[26] Cyprian, *De Unitate Ecclesiae*, 6 (PL 3, 503).

[27] The internal citation is from: Benedict XVI, *Deus Caritas Est*, n. 14.

be more pleasing to God than a life which appears outwardly in order, but moves through the day without confronting great difficulties'" (AL 305; EG 44).

Nevertheless, to understand the difficulties and the limitations that persons may have is not to suggest that the Church could have authority over basic principles of the moral law and that she should adapt the law to what people think that they can accomplish. This suggestion would be altogether contrary to the Pope's thought, inasmuch as he himself emphasizes in another passage that "gradualness is not in the law itself (cf. *Familiaris consortio*, 34)," and that this is why "discernment can never prescind from the Gospel demands of truth and charity, as proposed by the Church" (AL 300). In his view, therefore, discernment must occur according to the truth and according to Church teaching. Moreover, the proposal to allow for gradualness of the law is one of the clearest expressions of what Francis denounces as the failure "to inspire trust in God's grace" (AL 36). The most obvious reason why we do not *inspire* trust in God's grace is that often we do not *have* this trust to begin with. The Holy Father seems therefore to have in mind the neo-Pelagianism which afflicts a large part of the Church and which unfortunately has spread even in some national hierarchies. It reduces moral theology to philosophical ethics. The practical requirements of the Gospel-way-of-life are seen as the cogitations of an abstract reason or the impositions of an arbitrary will, with which human beings must cope by placing their trust in their own powers. For today's neo-Pelagians, the law is not the expression of the wisdom of a benevolent Father who invites us to be his friends. For them, there is no sanctifying grace to count on; we must fulfill the law by relying on our own resources, and the only way to do that is to adapt the law to what we consider to be our concrete possibilities. Thus they seek every possible way of lightening the burden of the law on people's consciences, for fear that the faithful might become discouraged. The Pope is rightly critical of a modern moral "theology" that has forgotten to be theology. Abstract rules, arbitrarily imposed and detached from any context of God's salvific love for every human being, can in fact become stones to be hurled at people (cf. AL 305).

What is no doubt necessary (and Pope Francis encourages it) is a return to the primacy of charity: "Special care should always be shown to emphasize and encourage the highest and most central values of the Gospel, particularly the primacy of charity" (AL 311). Charity, that is to say "a certain friendship of man for God,"[28] is in fact the key to understanding Christian moral life, including family morality. God loves us and offers us his friendship. He makes us his children and transforms us from within. His plan for our lives is good and within our grasp with the help of his grace. To the extent that marital morality involves obligations, they make sense inasmuch as they are "born of love itself" (AL 131). Therefore "the indissolubility of marriage . . . should not be viewed as a 'yoke' imposed on humanity, but as a 'gift' granted to those who are joined in marriage" (AL 62). We see that here indissolubility is clearly presented as a good that is really present and not as an abstract ideal. In the sacrament the spouses received this good as a gift conferred by Christ's grace. Any view of the persons' possibilities needs to count on this grace.

In his teaching on marriage, Jesus does not fall into the casuistry of the Pharisees; rather, claiming for himself greater authority than that of Moses, he proclaims "the meaning of marriage as the fullness of revelation that restores God's original plan" (AL 62). How can he claim this authority? How can he think that this "hardness of heart," which was Moses' reason for permitting divorce, is no longer a reason to undermine God's original plan? The fact is that Jesus is the new Moses who not only gives a law as Moses did but also does something that Moses could not do: Jesus not only gives the law; he gives us also the ability to fulfill it. Hence the New Law "makes us comply freely with these precepts and prohibitions, inasmuch as we do so through the promptings of grace."[29] Christ gives us a new heart. His grace is efficacious. Therefore marriage as a sacrament, as an efficacious sign of grace

---

[28] Thomas Aquinas, *Summa theologiae*, II–II, q. 23, art. 1. Francis too understands charity in the Thomistic sense of the love of friendship for God when he writes: "After the love that unites us to God, conjugal love is the 'greatest form of friendship'" (AL 123).

[29] Thomas Aquinas, *Summa theologiae*, I–II, q. 108, art. 1, ad 2.

that makes present Christ's love for his bride, the Church, "is not a social convention, an empty ritual or merely the outward sign of a commitment" (AL 72). That would be a merely human way of seeing it. Rather, "the sacrament is a gift given for the sanctification and salvation of the spouses" (AL 72). Therefore, in order to defend the indissolubility of marriage—a consequence of the fact that it is a sacrament—it is necessary to help it "to grow ever stronger under the impulse of grace" (AL 134).

God's grace, of course, always remains active, and it is necessary to place our trust in it also in situations that are difficult, irregular, or, objectively speaking, sinful. In these cases the Pope calls for discernment that "must help to find possible ways of responding to God and growing in the midst of limits" (AL 305). He speaks about a "divine pedagogy" by means of which "the Church turns with love to those who participate in her life in an imperfect manner: she seeks the grace of conversion for them; she encourages them to do good, to take loving care of each other and to serve the community in which they live and work" (AL 78). He dedicates all of chapter eight to the question of how to "accompany, discern, and integrate weakness." Obviously all this would make no sense if there were no hope that persons can change (cf. AL 116) and that under the influence of grace they can in fact convert (cf. AL 78). There would be no reason to accompany them, and most importantly there would be nothing to discern.

Some suggest that the repercussions of the indissolubility of marriage are unbearable burdens. They maintain that the most urgent task of pastoral care of the family is to establish binding criteria to regulate the admission to the sacraments of divorced persons who have remarried civilly. In this way they give the impression that *for them the main problem is not the new union, but the norms of canon law*. Consequently the solution too will be obvious, from their perspective: Change canon law and the problem will be resolved. By no longer insisting on the need for the divorced and civilly remarried to change their lifestyle before being readmitted to the sacraments, the Church would be telling them that there is nothing wrong with their situation and that the problem resides instead in an outmoded juridical norm. She would likewise imply that the sixth commandment, "Thou shalt not commit adultery," is basically an invention of canon law that the Church has full authority to change and adapt.

However, *adapting the moral law to what we consider to be our abilities is not a pastoral action. It is a legal action aimed at making pastoral activity superfluous.* It likewise expresses a lack of faith in God, whose grace enables us to be faithful to the Gospel way of life. Let us imagine for a moment that Pope Francis, hypothetically, had in fact decided to resolve by means of a redefinition of God's plan the problem posed by those whose way of life is objectively and publicly in contradiction with that plan (as though he had intended to say: "It is enough to make a few efforts, and even a second, third, or fourth union will be fine, provided that we admit that this is not exactly the ideal"). In that case he would not have had to write chapter eight of *Amoris laetitia*. What need would there be to accompany, discern, and integrate if the persons were basically doing fine and if all that was required was to adjust a few outmoded juridical norms?

There are, indeed, few other areas in life in which we are inclined to think in this way. We could ask ourselves, by analogy, whether the problem with illegal drug trafficking lies in the fact that it is illegal or in the fact that it is drug trafficking. In the first case, the problem would disappear the moment drug trafficking became legal. Here, as elsewhere, the problem is a nominalistic morality that does not see the law as an ordinance of reason,[30] but as the imposition of a superior will on a subordinate. According to this approach, the law does not need to be understood: it needs to be obeyed—because otherwise we will be punished. Merciful legislators adjust the law to the abilities of their own subordinates and perhaps sometimes refrain from punishing them for their failings. All the while the law is nothing but a function of their will. Since the law is imposed arbitrarily, it can be modified arbitrarily, given that it has no reference to truth or reason. For this type of

[30] Cf. Thomas Aquinas, *Summa theologiae*, I–II, q. 90, art. 4: "Rationis ordinatio ad bonum commune, ab eo qui curam communitatis habet, promulgata." "An ordinance of reason for the common good, made by him who has care of the community, and promulgated."

morality it suffices to say that the second, third, or fourth union of divorced persons who have remarried civilly is a good thing, and the problem of the divorced and civilly remarried will be resolved.

This, however, is not Pope Francis' approach. He emphasizes that "the law is itself a gift of God which points out the way, a gift for everyone without exception" (AL 295). Consequently, by saying that the law points out the way, he compares it to road signs. Those of us who had to drive before the advent of satellite navigation systems will still appreciate the gift-character of road signs. They are not arbitrary impositions, but an aid that helps us to arrive where we really want to go. If I want to go to Milan and come across road signs that point in the opposite direction from the one in which I am traveling, I have two options: I can turn the road signs around or I can turn the car around. Only one of the two options will bring me to Milan. Since the moral law points out the road to our true destination by expressing the truth about our authentic good, the idea of adjusting it to our abilities makes as much sense as the idea of turning the road signs around to point in the direction in which there is less traffic or a smoother highway. Such an option betrays a very pessimistic view of the human person and of grace. Since we cannot trust in God's grace but are compelled to do it on our own, we must adjust the law so as not to fall into complete desperation and total lawlessness.

Pope Francis, on the contrary, reminds us about God's grace when he discusses the topic of "conjugal charity" as "the love between husband and wife" that is "enriched and illuminated by the grace of the sacrament of marriage" (AL 120). Moreover, he warns pastors of souls that discernment of these situations must be carried out carefully, "for the sake of truth" (AL 79; FC 84). We see, therefore, that Francis argues against a neo-Pelagian, voluntaristic position that sees the law as an arbitrary imposition to be observed on the basis of one's own efforts. In fact he reaffirms the constant teaching of the Church: even though every person has his or her own process of gradual growth, "gradualness is not in the law itself (cf. *Familiaris consortio*, 34)," and for this reason "discernment can never prescind from the Gospel demands of truth and charity, as proposed by the Church" (AL 300). The law springs from love (cf. AL 131) and can be understood as a road sign (cf. AL 295) that points out the way to our true destination: loving communion with God, the deepest source of meaning in our lives (cf. AL 320). Spouses are not left on their own. They can count on God's efficacious grace that is given to them in the sacrament that they have received.

3. THE GOAL OF DISCERNMENT

According to the Pope, "discernment must help to find possible ways of responding to God and growing in the midst of limits" (AL 305). This does not mean abandoning "God's plan in all its grandeur" (AL 307). In *Amoris laetitia* 300 we find what is perhaps the most elaborate definition of discernment. Here, Francis, repeating the results of the Synods, proposes at least seven characteristics of discernment, correctly understood:

a) It is a process that "guides the faithful to an awareness of their situation before God."
b) It "contributes to the formation of a correct judgment on what hinders the possibility of a fuller participation in the life of the Church."
c) It examines the steps that can foster this participation and make it grow.
d) It "can never prescind from the Gospel demands of truth and charity, as proposed by the Church."
e) It requires "humility, discretion and love for the Church and her teaching."
f) It promotes sincerity in the search for God's will and "a desire to make a more perfect response to it."
g) It involves the subordination of one's own desires to a concern for the common good of the Church.

We see therefore that the *goal* that discernment must set for itself is not to find the way to admit to Holy Communion everyone who wants to receive it. The purpose of discernment is not to find ways to get around ecclesiastical norms or to discover gaps in the law so as to satisfy persons and to give them what they want. If it were, then the problem would simply be the norms themselves, and the clearest, simplest solution would be to change those norms. Instead, discernment consists in helping persons to become aware of their situation in God's sight, in order to participate more fully in the life of the Church and to respond to God's will with sincerity, humility, and in conformity with the requirements of truth and charity. For them this in turn will mean going back to living according to the truth of their marriage bond. Indeed, what Francis wishes for the Church is precisely "a pastoral care . . . centred on the marriage bond" (AL 211), which contrasts with the "culture of the ephemeral" that he often denounces (cf. AL 39, 124). For the Pope, it is by helping persons to develop stable relationships that one works to "promote a culture of the family."[31]

The goal of discernment is therefore not to find exceptions, but to help those who are living in a new union to identify ways to live in fidelity to the marital promise that they have made to their spouse before God and before the Church. The problem lies not in the Church's canon law, nor in the moral law, but in the new union. And the problem with the new union, in turn, is not simply the fact that it is opposed to the ecclesiastical norms, but that it is opposed to the true good of everyone involved. The union itself is a wound that must be treated. The reason for pursuing this objective is not found in any sort of rigorism or legalism, but in the conviction that marital fidelity corresponds to the true good of the person. While the new union is a wound, the persons can come to their authentic flourishing, can truly love, give themselves, and receive themselves by living according to the truth of their situation, which in this case means living according to the truth of their marriage bond. The reason for proposing this goal is found also in the conviction that with God's grace the persons are in fact

[31] Cf. Francis, *Address to the Bishops of the Episcopal Conference of Austria on their ad limina Visit* (January 30, 2014).

capable of acting in this way. Therefore, as already mentioned in the first chapter, the Council of Trent insists that, with the help of God's grace, it really is possible for Christians to keep the Ten Commandments, including the Sixth.[32] Vatican Council II declares that the vocation to holiness is not just for some professional Christians, but for all the faithful.[33] All are called to the perfection of charity and therefore, as a matter of principle, are capable of living in a way that corresponds to it.[34] Therefore, even in situations of failure and objective difficulties, even if the spouses are sinning seriously against each other, to the point where they have to separate temporarily, they will be capable of maintaining their mutual fidelity. Through God's grace they will be in principle capable of honoring their mutual promise, which was born of an authentic love, a love that "hopes all things" (1 Cor 13:7; cf. AL 116). After all, their promise did not consist of asserting that they would always get along together, or that they would never go through serious conflicts. Rather, their words of consent implied the promise never to despair of one another, even if one of the spouses had sinned seriously against the other. Their words imply the promise never to lose hope in the other, "realizing that reconciliation is a possibility" (AL 238) and knowing that the other spouse "can change, mature and radiate unexpected beauty and untold potential" (AL 116).

---

[32] Cf. Council of Trent, *Decree on Justification*, Session 6, chapter 11, *DH* 1536: "No one, however much he be justified, should consider himself exempt from the observance of the commandments [*can. 20*]; and no one should say that the observance of God's commandments is impossible for the man justified—a rash statement censured by the Fathers with anathema [*cann. 18 and 22; cf. *397*]. 'For God does not command the impossible, but when he commands he admonishes you to do what you can and to pray for what you cannot do, and he helps you to be able to do it.'"

[33] Cf. Second Vatican Council, *Lumen gentium*, n. 39: "Therefore all in the Church, whether they belong to the hierarchy or are cared for by it, are called to holiness."

[34] Cf. Ibid., n. 40: "It is therefore quite clear that all Christians in any state or walk of life are called to the fullness of Christian life and to the perfection of love, and by this holiness a more human manner of life is fostered also in earthly society."

4. THE METHOD OF DISCERNMENT: THINKING WITH THE CHURCH

In his rules for choosing and discerning, St. Ignatius of Loyola distinguishes between questions about which it is possible to make choices and those about which choices cannot be made. He observes therefore that "it is necessary that all matters of which we wish to make a choice be either indifferent or good in themselves, and such that they are lawful within our Holy Mother, the hierarchical Church, and not bad or opposed to her."[35] There can be a question of discernment about whether or not to make a trip to the mountains, but no discernment will be necessary or possible about whether or not to kill an innocent person. Choices are not required with regard to bad actions. We know from the start that they must not and cannot be chosen. Furthermore, "there are things that fall under an unchangeable choice, such as the priesthood, marriage, etc."[36] In the case of a choice of this type, "[since] an unchangeable choice, once it has been made, . . . cannot be undone, no further choice is possible."[37] If I am married, I do not need to discern whether I want to continue to be married. My marriage is not in question. The problem, rather, concerns the new union apart from my marriage. This is the wound and the affliction. In this case it becomes necessary to discern ways to return to the truth of one's own "situation before God" (AL 300). Therefore the goal of returning to a lifestyle that is in keeping with the truth of the marriage bond is not in itself an object of discernment, but rather delineates the context in which discernment can be carried out in a meaningful way.

Discernment likewise has a *method*. In order to discern correctly, we need to think with the Church (*sentire cum ecclesia*), as St. Ignatius says. This requires humility, docility, and sincerity. Therefore among his "Rules for Thinking with the Church Mil-

[35] *The Spiritual Exercises of St. Ignatius*, a new translation by Louis J. Puhl, S.J., n. 170, p. 72.

[36] Ibid., n. 171, p. 72.

[37] Ibid., n. 172, p. 72.

itant," we read that "We must put aside all judgment of our own, and keep the mind ever ready and prompt to obey in all things the true Spouse of Christ our Lord, our holy Mother, the hierarchical Church."[38] For Ignatius, to think with the Church also means to "praise all the commandments of the Church, and be on the alert to find reasons to defend them, and by no means in order to criticize them."[39] To discern, therefore, does not mean to justify every conceivable desire in the absence of reasons. It means, rather, to seek reasons that correspond to the requirements of truth and charity.

Now that the goal and the method of discernment have been clarified, we can move on to the actual practice of it. We would like to propose at least three objects of discernment:

a) the discernment of *desire*,
b) the discernment of the *marriage bond*, and
c) the discernment of particular lines of *conduct* and of useful *practices*.

In the next section we will deal with each of these.

5. THE OBJECTS OF DISCERNMENT

a. Discerning desire

In speaking about the discernment of desire, Pope Francis makes reference to our Lord himself, who in his encounter with the Samaritan woman "addressed her desire for true love, in order to free her from the darkness in her life and to bring her to the full joy of the Gospel" (AL 294). Jesus offers the woman living water, an inexhaustible spring that will definitively quench the thirst of anyone who drinks of it. She is immediately interested:

[38] Ibid., n. 353, p. 157.
[39] Ibid., n. 361, p. 158.

"The woman said to him, 'Sir, give me this water, that I may not thirst, nor come here to draw'" (Jn 4:15). Her desire for her own source of water is actually quite understandable. A private well would resolve one of her biggest problems. Her difficulty is not that she has to draw water. Everyone in her city must do this. Her problem is that she has to come at *midday* (cf. Jn 4:6), when the sun beats harshly in a way that is difficult to imagine for anyone accustomed to the more temperate climates of the northern skies. Jesus immediately takes another step forward, revealing that the woman's difficulty is not primarily the fact of having to come at midday, but rather the reason *why* she has to come at midday. He therefore tells her: "Go, call your husband, and come here" (Jn 4:16), and we learn from her response that she has no husband, while Jesus himself reminds her that she has had five husbands and is now living in a free union. This is the reason why she usually comes at midday: she wants to avoid other people who might scorn her as a public sinner. Jesus very gently brings her to ask the right questions: *Why* do I desire what I desire? *What* do I *truly* desire? What is the deeper problem that prevents me from having what I desire?

The woman's first reaction to the fundamental questions that Jesus poses to her is exactly what one would expect from most people of our time when they come to speak about existential questions: she dodges. She actually shifts the discussion to a more abstract and theoretical level. How does she connect the question about the proper place of worship to the reality of living with a man to whom she is not married? There is no connection. And this is precisely why she brought up the topic. With great delicacy once again, Jesus avoids being drawn into a theological discussion, shifts his attention to a higher plane ("the true worshipers will worship the Father in spirit and truth" [Jn 4:23]) and also tells her something very important about himself, which he was rather reluctant to reveal publicly on other occasions ("I who speak to you am he," i.e., the Messiah [Jn 4:26]). At these words, the Samaritan woman abandons her initial mission. She leaves the jar of water behind and runs toward her city. No longer afraid of her fellow citizens, she tells them about Jesus. At this point she reveals what truly touched her. It was not their theological discussion but the existential and moral discourse that had a direct impact on her life: "Come, see a man who told me all that I ever did. Can this be the Christ?" (Jn 4:29). Jesus spoke to her true desire, to her heart. The problem is at the existential level, concerning what she did, and the living water that Jesus offered her is a solution to precisely this problem. It is not an external solution that only resolves the problem of having to leave the house at midday. It is a true remedy that goes to the heart of the problem. There is no longer need to be ashamed: reconciliation is possible, and in fact it has already begun, as can be seen by the fact that the woman intentionally seeks the people whom she had so carefully sought to avoid and by the fact that these people truly listen to her, believe her, and go to Jesus.

In the case of divorced persons in a new union who wish to receive the Eucharist, pastors can help with the discernment of this desire in a similar way. In their efforts to accompany the people in question, they will have to ask what this desire to receive the Eucharist is based upon. For some, this desire might simply be based on the fact that, on account of their objective living situation, they are not admitted. They would have no desire to receive the Eucharist if they were allowed to. They find it very annoying that there is something they are not authorized to do, however insignificant it might seem to them. These people are similar to those who have never once cast a vote in the elections of their own country, but who adamantly affirm their right to vote in the country where they live as resident aliens. In their case, having the right is more important than what the right allows them to do. What is desired here is not the Eucharist in a strict sense, but the *right* to receive it.

How should persons with this sort of desire for rights be accompanied? How does one build on these suppositions? It can be difficult to build something on a desire of this sort. Pastors can try to help these people to appreciate the divine economy of grace and mercy, which follows a logic that is diametrically opposed to the human economy of rights. It is not advisable for any soul to approach the judgment seat of God and to assert her rights before the King of kings. May God spare us from receiving what is ours by right. The best things in life are not owed to us by right. For starters, our existence itself is not something we could have reasonably claimed by right. It did not have to be. It did not have to be this way. Since the right of one person always presupposes a corresponding obligation of another person, generally we do not have the *right* to get married or to be friends with someone. After all, no one has the *duty* to marry us or to be our friend. *A fortiori*, no creature could assert a right in relation to God. A right to grace is an obvious oxymoron because grace is freely given by its very definition. The first thing to say to those who assert rights is that the Eucharist is the body of Christ. It is not something trite. No one has a right to receive it. Many people cannot or should not receive it, even if they are publicly admitted, since they eat and drink their own condemnation. And while non-admission will seem unjust if it is perceived as arbitrary, the fact is that it is based on objective reasons. In order to make these reasons comprehensible, a renewed catechetical effort will be necessary and helpful. Some of the following considerations could be clarified: it is necessary to discern the body of Christ in the mystery of the Church in order to discern the body of Christ in the mystery of the Eucharist; the Church springs from the Eucharist; receiving the Eucharist is not just a private matter between Jesus and me; there is a unity in the sacramental order; one's life in the body represents a sign; one sacrament (the Eucharist) cannot be received in contradiction with another (marriage); non-admission implies no judgment about the state of grace of one's soul; there are other people too who cannot receive the Eucharist, without this implying any judgment about the state of their souls: for example, catechumens or little children.

For some divorced persons who live in a new extramarital union, their desire to receive the Eucharist comes from a sense of embarrassment at the time for communion. Everyone gets up for the altar call. Not presenting oneself at the Eucharistic table is perceived as being exposed as a public sinner. They might even prefer not going to Mass at all rather than remaining in the pew while everyone else goes forward. Their very understandable desire is not to feel embarrassed at Mass. The simplest way to avoid embarrassment might seem to be allowing them to go up and receive the Lord. And while it may be true that the Church's practice of not admitting the divorced and "remarried" to the sacraments also serves to remind them that all is not well, that is, it also has the purpose of helping them avoid settling too easily into a situation that is not good for them or for the Church, the objective is clearly not to embarrass them once a week.

One way of responding to this justified desire might be better catechesis on the Eucharist for the entire parish. Here, for example, questions about worthy reception can be addressed, and it can be emphasized that the sacrament is certainly a sacrament of healing for our daily weaknesses (cf. AL 305, note 351) and our nourishment for fighting against sin and working toward sanctity. However, it will also need to be emphasized that every deliberate act involving grave matter defined by the Ten Commandments is such that it prevents the reception of the Lord in a worthy manner. Consequently, the more one wishes to highlight the healing power of the Eucharist, the more one must reveal the importance of the Sacrament of Penance.

In addition to a greater catechetical effort, the pros and cons of what is a common practice in at least some countries might be weighed: that is, an invitation for *everyone* to come up at the time of the distribution of the Eucharist, having previously established a particular gesture—such as folding both arms over the chest—as a way of indicating one's desire to receive only a blessing and not the sacramental species.

Among the divorced and civilly remarried there are certainly also those whose desire to receive the Eucharist based primarily on the fact that they love the Lord. They know that the Eucharist signifies an intimate union with the Lord, which is what they truly desire. This is obviously a very positive desire. And once again much headway can be made with appropriate catechesis. Usually the faithful who have this type of desire are among the first to see the reasonableness of the Church's practice, particularly when they have understood that the celebration of the Eucharist, inasmuch as it is a sacrament, is an ecclesial act that is not carried out only between Jesus and the soul of the individual. They can come to understand that their objective situation, independently of their state of grace, is in contradiction with the mystery of Christ's fidelity to his spouse, the Church. Their desire for union with Christ can therefore mature into a desire to change their lifestyle. The fact that they are not admitted to receive Communion will prevent them in any case from feeling comfortable with their situation. The Church's practice reminds them that there is something awry. As an aside, this is an act of mercy and not of accusation. It is an act of mercy to remind someone with a broken leg or an open wound that something is not right and then to encourage the person to seek help and to find the way to promote healing.

b. Discerning the marriage bond

While St. Ignatius observes that once a couple is married there is no longer need to discern the married state—which means there is no longer any need to reflect on whether or not to get married, because the matter is settled—the question of whether one has in fact validly contracted marriage can of course be posed reasonably even after the wedding. Some have implicitly suggested that a solution to the problem of the divorced and civilly remarried could be found in the question regarding the nullity of marriage. In fact, as far as they are concerned, if the Church would only "grant" annulments on a larger scale, the problem of divorced persons who have remarried civilly would disappear in practice.

There are several things to say about this proposal. Given the highly misleading nature of the term "annulment," it is extremely important to emphasize that a declaration of nullity is not a dispensation, but a judgment issued by the public ecclesial authority stating that a marriage bond did not in fact exist from the beginning. A declaration of nullity therefore is not a *solution* to anything but rather an indication of a grave *problem*. Why were the presumed spouses not capable of contracting a valid marriage? Where did the grave limitations on their freedom or the grave defects of their will come from?

Discernment of the matrimonial bond should not be seen therefore as a means of allowing divorced and civilly remarried persons to marry in the Church and thereby regain access to the sacraments. Rather, discerning one's marriage bond is part of what Pope Francis calls the discernment of one's "situation before God" (AL 300). It will serve to shed light on the question of whether or not I am truly married, and this clarification in itself has an existential significance for me. Given the social and ecclesial nature of marriage, this discernment must be public and ecclesial, and it will certainly help me to face my future. If I was not in fact married and if the causes for the invalidity of my marriage attempt were independent of me, or no longer apply, I can feel free to try again to find a spouse. If I really am married, I know that I continue to be bound to my spouse, even if we are separated and even if my spouse has been unfaithful to me and has entered into a new union. The main problem that a declaration of nullity aims to resolve is therefore the question of the status of one's marriage bond, and not the problem of Communion for the divorced and "remarried."

Keeping all of this in mind, obviously it will often be reasonable for pastors to encourage divorced persons in a new union to discern—in the external forum through a regular canonical process—whether or not they are in fact bound to someone else by the bond of marriage. Nevertheless, since what is being sought is not a favor from the Church ("Let's find out whether the Church might grant you an annulment") but rather an objective judgment ("Let's find out, with the help of the ecclesial tribunal, whether or not you are actually married to someone"), it seems that there should be at least some apparent reasons for thinking that perhaps the marriage truly was not valid if this route is to be encouraged. It is another matter if there are no such reasons, and if one or both spouses are convinced in conscience that their marriage was actually contracted validly, even if they found it necessary to separate and even if one or both now live together with someone else. To say it again: a declaration of nullity is not the solution to a problem. It is the public declaration of a problem: an attempt at marriage was made and was not successful. This is not good news.

Suppose that a husband does not share his wife's conviction that their marriage is null. Could there not be some circumstances in which he perceives the declaration of nullity as a declaration that the love of his life was in reality the lie of his life? And what about the children they had together? Might they not perceive that in this way the ecclesial authority has notified them that they are not the fruit of a great love but of a big farce? Considering these sometimes catastrophic consequences of a declaration of nullity, it is absolutely necessary that the declaration be based on objective facts and not on a misinterpreted feeling of kindness or mercy. Indeed, this is not good news. No doubt there is a great deal of bad news we will have to face in our lives. It may be that among the bad news one would have to include the fact that what one thought was one's marriage never actually was a marriage. The sadness and suffering entailed in recognizing such a fact show that the question of discerning the matrimonial bond must always address the question about the truth of the situation. It is better to live in the truth than to live a lie, even if the truth is unpleasant. Therefore, people can be grateful to the ecclesial tribunal for discerning their matrimonial bond, even if there may be bad news in the end. In order to discern well, however, the ecclesial authority must keep in mind that the declaration of nullity is not a gift, but a tragedy.

c. Discerning concrete steps

i. Reconciliation of the spouses

Having discussed the discernment of desire and the discernment of the matrimonial bond, now it is time to examine some concrete steps for helping people "to find possible ways of responding to God and growing in the midst of limits" (AL 305), to reach "an awareness of their situation before God" (AL 300), and ultimately to live according to the truth of their matrimonial bond. The first question that a "pastoral care . . . centred on the marriage bond" (AL 211) obviously has to ask is whether *reconciliation* is possible. Since "forgiveness is possible" (AL 106), in principle reconciliation should also be possible, although clearly reconciliation—unlike forgiveness—does not depend only on oneself but also on the other person, so it is never guaranteed. Nonetheless, it is obviously quite reasonable to ask whether the partners in a new union can abandon that union and return to their legitimate spouses. We are often too quick to rule out this possibility. The supporters of Church recognition for extramarital unions (after all, this is what the question of admitting the divorced and "remarried" to Communion boils down to) often present moving stories of bad luck and second chances as arguments. Why not put a seal of ecclesiastical approval on the new union, admitting the partners to communion and—as a logical next step—blessing their union? We forget the other stories about those who, after being unjustly abandoned, have remained faithful to the love of their life and have not given up hope for their spouse, believing that "human beings can experience conversion; they must never despair of being able to change their lives."[40] Some, in fact, have welcomed their spouse back again in moving circumstances. Others continue to live out their solitude not as a way of honoring an external and abstract norm of canon law, but as a way of loving the spouse to whom they had entrusted their life and as a way of loving God, before whom they made this promise. Not all of these stories have ended or will end in reconciliation. But some do; some even after years of separation and spousal infidelity.

If the Church were to recognize the new unions—which, we must not forget, seal the separation, definitively eliminate the hope of reconciliation and institutionalize marital infidelity—it would deal a severe blow to those whom the Church is called to care for the most: the weak, the abandoned, people who are alone, the poor in spirit, who with a humble attitude of serene surrender entrust their fate to God's Providence, who lament the loss of an unfaithful spouse and pray every day for the conversion and return of that spouse. A new union is not a solution. It does not resolve the tragedy of all that a broken marriage entails. At stake here is the very meaning of the persons' lives. Individuals

[40] Francis, *Message for the Celebration of the World Day of Peace,* January 1, 2014.

are traumatized by separation from a spouse and by habitual infidelity. These are issues that cause some people to commit suicide or to kill others or to lose their minds, thus losing their social standing, their life, and possibly their soul. Imagine a wife who has just been abandoned by her husband. She finds herself in an existential tragedy that worsens exponentially when she learns that he has begun to live with another woman and that therefore the chances of reconciliation are greatly reduced. If the ecclesial authority now recognizes and publicly approves the husband's new union, inviting him and his new partner to receive Communion or even blessing the new union, would not the wife who has been unjustly abandoned be justified in accusing the Church of complicity in the ruining of her life? Would not the Church become an enemy of the poor? If her pastor now suggested that it was time for her also to move on with her life and to find another partner (after all, the juridical question of the annulment can be solved), would this not seem cynical in view of the real tragedy she has just experienced? The task that the Church received from the Lord is to be the champion of the poor. Since she has a preferential option for the poor, she will take the part of the abandoned. Consequently, the Church will do everything possible to call the unfaithful spouse to conversion and will work to the best of her ability for the future reconciliation of the spouses.

ii. Abandoning the extramarital union

In the context of a pastoral care of the marriage bond, the goal of discernment is to identify ways in which the divorced persons who are living in an extramarital union can come to live in accordance with the truth of their situation: "Priests have the duty to 'accompany [the divorced and remarried] in helping them to understand their situation according to the teaching of the Church and the guidelines of the bishop'" (AL 300). And in fact "this discernment can never prescind from the Gospel demands of truth and charity, as proposed by the Church" (AL 300). The demands of truth require that divorced persons live in accordance with the truth of their indissoluble marriage bond. The demand of charity refers also to charity toward their spouse, from whom they are now separated but to whom they owe—out of love and justice—an attitude of hope for the spouse's conversion and for a possible reconciliation, even in cases where reconciliation is unlikely. These requirements of truth and charity would clearly be fulfilled optimally if the spouses were to be reconciled. If reconciliation is not possible, then the best alternative way of fulfilling these demands would be to abandon any extramarital union in which they have become involved. In this way they can begin to live again—even individually—the good of fidelity to their marriage bond, which does not mean fidelity to a metaphysical abstraction but to one's spouse, who was and is the love of the person's life, even if they are still separated and reconciliation seems impossible at the moment.

In fact, with regard to the divorced and "remarried," St. Pope John Paul II and Francis speak of the general "obligation to separate," even though there may be serious particular circumstances that make the persons in question unable to fulfill the obligation, exempting them from it (cf. FC 84; AL 298). The reasons that would exonerate them from the moral obligation to separate are subject to discernment. While *Familiaris consortio* 84 and *Amoris laetitia* 298 speak of "serious reasons, such as the children's upbringing," the Apostolic Exhortation *Sacramentum Caritatis* by Benedict XVI is less specific, speaking only of "objective circumstances [that] make it impossible to cease cohabitation" (SC 29). Common children, the responsibility of having to care for a sick partner, obligations deriving from intricate financial situations can be good motives for not separating. However, within the context of discerning reasons that would dispense from the moral obligation to abandon the extramarital union, it should be kept in mind that not every *thinkable* reason is necessarily a *good* reason.

iii. Ways of living in abstinence

If for serious reasons abandoning the extramarital union turns out to be impossible, then the minimum requirement for satisfying the demands of truth and charity is observing abstinence. In this way, two people who share a house without being married in

God's sight abstain from sharing the same bed, renouncing those acts which are proper to spouses. After all, the partners in the new extramarital union are *not* spouses. Anyone who believes in the fundamental principles of logic and the distinctive characteristics of marriage, such as indissolubility and exclusivity, must admit this fact.

It has been called into question, even by some national hierarchies, whether practicing abstinence is possible for ordinary believers. Consequently, some maintain that the moral requirement of living in permanent continence is nothing other than a largely impracticable counsel, since it is equivalent to choosing a form of celibate life, to which the persons in question do not feel called. Nonetheless, we need to consider that from the Old to the New Testament, from the Apostolic Age to our own, "Thou shalt not commit adultery" has never been considered a counsel, but a command. And it has been consistently interpreted as referring to all sexual relations that are not conjugal, whether premarital or extramarital.

Since the Gospel is addressed to all human beings, its moral demands are also addressed to all. With regard to the Sixth Commandment, someone who is separated from his or her spouse, whether or not a new union has been established, is in the same situation as someone who is not yet married or will never be married, for whatever reason. We are not talking about just a handful of people. Even within marriage situations can arise that prevent the spouses from uniting for extended periods of time. Suppose that one of them has to go on a long business trip. Should the other perhaps say, "I'm not called to the religious life," and look for a short-term lover to compensate for the absence of the spouse? And what if one of them became sick in such a way as to make it physically impossible for them to have sexual relations ever again? Could the healthy partner be advised to seek out occasional substitutes or even to abandon the sick spouse on the grounds of not being called to the celibate life? Of course, abstinence—whether temporary or permanent—is difficult. But it does not follow that celibacy cannot be commanded in certain circumstances, or that it cannot be a requirement of love and justice.

Several very concrete steps of discernment come into play here. Since abstinence is difficult, discernment will ask how abstinence can be made possible, even between a man and a woman who have affection for each other and share the same house even though they are not married in God's sight. Plainly a strong resolution is needed in order to do something difficult, and this in turn requires an understanding of the reasons for what one is attempting to do. No one will accomplish anything difficult without understanding why it is reasonable, suitable, and good. Abstinence in the present context is not a demand of an abstract law arbitrarily placed by the clergy on the shoulders of the lay faithful. It is rather a requirement of the love that one has for one's own spouse. *A spouse remains bound not to a far-off metaphysical idea but to a concrete person, who is loved and to whom the spouse has promised his or her own life before God.* As difficult as the reminder may be, and as understandable as the desire to forget and leave everything behind may be, practicing abstinence in an extramarital union will require deliberate efforts to remember the reason for this practice: one's legitimate spouse.

With regard to very concrete steps that can be taken in terms of these efforts to remember, pastors together with the faithful in question will have to exercise careful discernment, conscious of the fact that some may have experienced profound psychological trauma that will require special procedures and even the help of specialists. Nevertheless, healing the memory will be possible in principle; a point can be reached where it is possible to remember one's spouse without reliving any trauma that may have been inflicted. In any case, pretending not to really be married will not help. That would mean merely closing one's eyes to reality, which ultimately would strike back with a vengeance. It is therefore necessary to discern ways of recognizing the reality of one's own life, which is to say: ways of remembering one's proper spouse within the limits of one's ability—clearly avoiding the risks of bringing back psychological trauma. One might ask whether the people in question could keep a picture of their legitimate spouse. Perhaps they could commit to saying a daily prayer for him or her. This will make present to them the reason for their abstinence:

loving fidelity to their spouse, however much he or she may have sinned against them. In this way they will allow Christ to love their spouse through them, loving their spouse with the very love of God that is poured out into their hearts through the Holy Spirit who has been given to them (cf. Rom 5:5).

Once there is a clear awareness of the reason for abstaining, the priest in the confessional needs to discern the will of the penitent. Is the person ready to take the next concrete step, which is the commitment to a life of abstinence? While growth in virtue is gradual, conversion is sudden: it is "yes" or "no." In the case under discussion, conversion means the firm determination of the will to live in union with Christ, to desire and imitate him. It entails the desire to be transformed into his likeness and the firm resolution to change one's lifestyle wherever it contradicts the very nature of Christ. Just as Jesus is unconditionally faithful to his bride, the Church, so I want to be faithful to my spouse, even if she has been or is unfaithful to me. I want to do everything in my power to separate from any other lovers and to be reconciled with her. If I am unable to reconcile with my spouse, and if it is not possible to separate from my lover without committing a grave injustice, then at the least I will abstain from those acts which are proper to spouses in the new union, thereby expressing my fidelity to and love for my true spouse. This is the moment of conversion. Here there is no gradualness. Therefore a priest who accompanies someone who is divorced and "remarried" needs to discern whether he or she is capable of promising what has been discussed here. If so, the person can receive absolution and can be admitted to the sacraments (while taking appropriate precautions to avoid scandal). If not, the priest should not harshly deny absolution, but simply postpone it until the penitent is ready.

Now let us suppose the partners in an extramarital union have made the commitment to live according to the truth of their situation, but now they fail to do what they had decided to do. Passion overcomes them, and they end up uniting even though they had decided not to. What can they do? They can repent and confess just like any other believer. And together with the priest they should discern the concrete steps that will help them live in accordance with their resolution. They should ask which practices and common activities help them remain faithful to their purpose and which do not. If they are sincerely determined to live according to the truth of their situation in God's sight, they will examine the circumstances that led them to act against their purpose and seek ways to avoid similar situations in the future. Their discernment will have a lot to do with examining and creating the right external conditions. In Jesus' parable of the wheat and the weeds, the farmer does not examine the insides of the seeds. He creates favorable conditions by cultivating the field (cf. Mt 13:24–30). In the same way, in their task of discernment, pastors need to give people the possibility of growing "in the midst of limits" (AL 305) by identifying and promoting suitable external conditions.

CONCLUSION

Discernment, therefore, does not consist in making exceptions to some general rules, but in finding ways to guide and accompany people along a path. Now, a path is a path only if there is a destination. Without an endpoint, people will not be travelling on a path; rather, they will merely be wandering around. The object of discernment is therefore not the destination in itself, but the way by which to arrive at it. Once I know that I want to go to Milan, I have many options for getting there, which will require careful discernment based on my concrete circumstances. Should I go by train, by plane, by car, or by horse? Maybe I could go on foot or ride a bike. I can take the interstate highway or local roads. It will depend on where I am (am I nearby or far away?) and on several particular personal circumstances (am I afraid of flying? Am I allergic to horses?). Since the discernment pertains to a way toward a destination, it is intimately bound up with accompaniment and integration. In order to travel on a road, light is necessary. To distinguish between left and right, to choose A or B in order to reach C, one needs an orientation and criteria. As we hope we have shown, there are essentially two lights that guide discernment: the truth of the marriage bond and the truth of the desire. In this way, priests can confidently carry out their "duty to 'accompany [the divorced and remarried] in helping them to understand their situation according to the teaching of the Church and the guidelines of the bishop'" (AL 300), helping them "to find possible ways of responding to God and growing in the midst of limits" (AL 305).